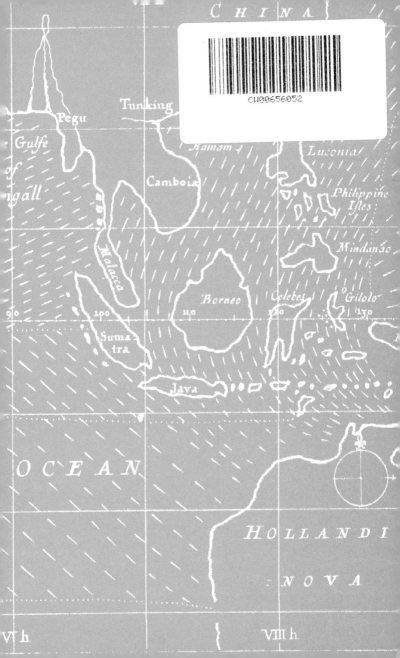

The
Female Shipwright

The

History of the

Female Shipwright

by Mary Lacy

with an introduction
by Margarette Lincoln

**NATIONAL
MARITIME
MUSEUM**

Original spelling, grammar and punctuation retained throughout.

First published in 1773

This edition published by
the National Maritime Museum, Greenwich, London SE10 9NF
www.nmm.ac.uk/publishing

Introduction © 2008, National Maritime Museum, Greenwich, London

ISBN 978-1-906367-01-5

A CIP catalogue record for this book is available from the British
Library.

Printed and bound in England
by Cromwell Press Ltd, Trowbridge, Wiltshire

Mixed Sources
Product group from well-managed
forests and other controlled sources
www.fsc.org Cert no. TT-COC-2082
© 1996 Forest Stewardship Council
FSC

CONTENTS

INTRODUCTION

by Margarette Lincoln

Mary Lacy was a remarkable woman. In an age when women did not serve in the armed forces or train to become qualified shipwrights or set themselves up as speculative house builders, Lacy did all three. Her story, published in 1773 when she was thirty-three, saw three editions. It should be set in the context of contemporary narratives describing 'female warriors' who dressed as men and went to sea, fighting and grappling with the elements alongside their shipmates. Their alleged motives were various: economic distress, a wish to be with their lover who had joined the navy or been impressed, or simply a desire to break free from social constraint. Ballads about cross-dressing women circulated in print as commercial songs from 1650 to about 1850. In the radical 1790s, feminists arguing for greater sexual equality cited them as examples of female bravery but such tales excited more popular than political interest.

Lacy's fascinating autobiography offers greater depth, giving rare and varied insights into working class life in the eighteenth century. We see glimpses of her rural upbringing and domestic service: her parents were poor, forced to work hard and had no time to supervise her upbringing strictly. She grew up wild and reckless so that her mother put her into service at the age of twelve to keep her off the streets. Lacy's account also reveals something of life on board a warship (her account of a storm at sea is frighteningly vivid), and the gruelling physical labour that went on behind the walls of a royal dockyard, 'our company was ordered to tear up an old forty-gun ship, which was so very difficult to take to pieces that I strained my loins in the attempt, the effects of which I felt very sensibly at night when I went home, for I could hardly stand and had no appetite to my victuals.' Her narrative also has strong local links with Kent, Chatham and Deptford.

Lacy led a hard life and, with the advantage of hindsight, was critical of her thoughtless, idle behaviour as a young girl, 'with proper care and industry, I should, in all probability, have escaped many of the unknown sorrows I afterwards suffered'. Yet under the cloak of moral guidance, her narrative of sexual concealment offers many salacious passages attractive to a popular audience.

Lacy puts her impulse to run away in men's dress down to an 'unsettled' frame of mind following an unhappy love affair with a young man. This may be little more than a smokescreen for lesbian tendencies, as is the culmination of her tale in conventional married domesticity. Lacy went to sea aged nineteen, taking the name of William Chandler and becoming a carpenter's apprentice on board the *Sandwich*. That a woman might spend months on a ship without her sex being discovered seems far-fetched today, but there are well-attested cases of women who served in the navy dressed in men's clothes. Britain was in the middle of the Seven Years War, the navy was desperate for men, few questions were asked of willing volunteers.

Conditions at sea were dreadful: Lacy contracted rheumatism by the time she was twenty, causing her joints and legs to swell so badly that she was unable to walk and had to be sent to Haslar naval hospital at Portsmouth. She recovered enough to return to sea but, during a spell ashore at Portsmouth when twenty-three, she seized the opportunity to apply to be a shipwright's apprentice. This was a standard seven-year apprenticeship that required skills in mechanical drawing, writing and arithmetic as well as the ability to carry out hard physical work. By 1770, she had the certificate and the means to earn a living wage.

In 1771 there was a terrible dockyard fire at Portsmouth and shipwrights then had to work a seventeen-hour day. This aggravated Lacy's rheumatism until she could work no longer. Pain and a 'false friend' compelled her to reveal her sex. Helped by a Mr Richardson, who may have been a solicitor, she applied for an Admiralty pension. Although she gave her true name, Mary Lacy, on the forms, in January 1772 the Admiralty granted her the pension due to 'Superannuated Shipwrights' of £20 a year for the rest of her life. She went to Deptford, the nearest dockyard to the centre of London, to collect her money and there met a Mr Slade, whom she claimed she later married. Her autobiography, published under the name Mary Slade from an address in King Street, Deptford, ends at this point.

No registration of her marriage has been found. But 'Mary Slade of King Street, Deptford', who we can take to have been Mary Lacy, moved into a new double-fronted house in Deptford with Elizabeth Slade in 1777. This house was at the centre of a terrace, which she had built herself and which, long afterwards, was known as 'Slade's Place'. The terrace survives in part at Nos 104–108 and 116–118 Deptford High Street. These five houses are all that remain from a row of ten built in 1775–84 on a large plot of freehold land that 'Mary Slade' bought for £480 in 1775. It is not clear where the money came from but it seems likely that she used her pension of £20 p.a. as security for a mortgage. She lived another twenty years and was buried at St Nicholas, Deptford, on 6 February 1795. After her death, 'Mary Slade' was described as a 'spinster and shopkeeper' and her property passed to Elizabeth's relatives. Given the designation 'spinster', it seems probable that Lacy took Elizabeth Slade's surname to pass as her sister.

Lacy was determined, intelligent and resourceful. In an age when there were few options for women, she managed to break out of poverty and, through her own efforts, achieved a comfortable lifestyle.

Further Reading

Cordingly, David, *Women Sailors and Sailors' Women: An Untold Maritime History* (Waterville, Maine, 2001)

Dugaw, D., 'Balladry's Female Warriors: Women, Warfare, and Disguise in the Eighteenth Century', *Eighteenth-Century Life*, 9:2 (1985), 1–20

Guillery, Peter, 'The Further Adventures of Mary Lacy', *The Georgian Group Journal*, X (2000), 61–9

Stark, Suzanne J., *Female Tars: Women Aboard Ship in the Age of Sail* (Annapolis, Maryland, 1996)

PREFACE

*T*he reality of the facts contained in the following History will, it is presumed, conduce in a great measure to recommend the perusal of it to the Public; and it will, I doubt not, with every candid and considerate reader, prove a sufficient apology for the inaccuracies of stile and sentiment which I may be justly chargeable with as the author, that I laboured under many inconveniences in collecting the various materials which compose it. The great number of incidents related therein are presented to public inspection in a plain and simple garb, that being judged the most suitable dress for a narrative of this kind.

The reader will find herein,

1. A circumstantial account of what happened to me during my childhood, wherein will appear many evident tokens of that restless and untractable disposition in an early period of life, which gave rise to all my succeeding adventures and misfortunes.

2. The method made use for leaving my parents, by disguising myself in man's apparel, principally for the sake of withdrawing myself from the company of a young man, for whom I found I had conceived too great an attachment, and who was the primary, though involuntary cause of my departure – The uncommon embarrassments and difficulties I struggled with during the first four years of my service, in order to conceal my sex when at sea, where I was almost continually in company with 700 men for that time, without incurring the least suspicion of being a woman: for which, and the many narrow escapes I afterwards had, I cannot but acknowledge myself indebted to the goodness of Divine Providence, who endued me with prudence and discretion to conduct myself under every circumstance, and carried me through all.

3. Of my serving seven years as an apprentice to a shipwright, with the numerous sufferings I endured from ill treatment under different masters, and the various scenes of immorality and profaneness my situation amongst sea-faring people made me a constant, though disgusted, witness to. And,

4. The hardships I went through in being forced to cross the water at Gosport in the most inclement of seasons for the space of five years and a half; the severe labour I was employed in since that time, attended with illness, amidst the dreadful apprehensions of a discovery of my sex through the baseness of the woman who betrayed me.

It will not be amiss to conclude this address by explaining my motives for endeavouring to be as frequently as possible in the company of women, in the way of courtship; which were, In the first place, to avoid the conversation of the men, which I need not observe, was amongst those of this class especially, in many respects very offensive to a delicate ear: and, 2ndly, For the sake of affording me a more agreeable repast amongst persons of my own sex, many of whom, I am sorry to say, were too much addicted to evil practices by their unlawful commerce with the other, as will on many occasions appear in the course of the story.

Deptford, July 1, 1773.
M. SLADE.

THE HISTORY OF
THE FEMALE SHIPWRIGHT

After mentioning my maiden name, which was MARY LACY, it will be proper to inform the reader, that I was born at Wickham, in the county of Kent, on the 12th of January, 1740; but had not been long in the world before my father and mother agreed to live at Ash, so that I knew little more of Wickham than I had learned from my parents, on which account Ash might almost be reckoned my native place.

My father and mother were poor, and forced to work very hard for their bread. They had one son and two daughters, of whom I was the eldest. At a proper time, my mother put me to school, to give me what learning she could, which kept me out of their way whilst they were at work; for being young, I was always in mischief; and my mother not having spare time sufficient to look after me, I had so much my own will, that when I came to have some knowledge, it was a difficult matter for them to keep me within proper bounds.

After I had learned my letters, I was admitted into a charity school, which was kept by one Mrs. R___n; and she, knowing my parents, took great pains to instruct me in reading. As I took my learning very fast, my mistress was the more careful of me; for she was indeed as a mother to me; and in these respects was more serviceable than my parents could possibly be. When I was old enough to learn to work, my mistress taught me to knit; which she perceiving me very fond of learning, employed me in knitting gloves, stockings, night-caps, and such sort of work, so that I soon perfected myself in it; which I was more encouraged to, as my mistress rewarded me for every piece of knitting, and all the money I earned she reserved in a little box; so that when I wanted any thing, she would buy it for me. Thus, by the help of God and good friends, I was no great charge to my parents; for being always at school, my mistress set me about all manner of work in the house; so that, though young, I was very handy, and in a way of improvement.

About this time I used to go on errands for my neighbours, and help them what I could; but that practice, by occasioning me to go pretty much abroad in the streets, became very prejudicial to me; for I was thereby addicted to all manner of mischief, as will appear by the following instance: There was one C___h___e Cipp___r, about my age, that lived in Ash, with whom, when I could get out, I always kept company, and, when together, did many unjustifiable actions; for one day we took it into our heads to purloin a bridle and saddle out of the stable of one Mr. John R___n, butcher at Ash, who kept a little horse in a field about half a mile from the town. This horse we caught, put the saddle and bridle on, and rode about the field till we were tired, and afterwards restored them to the place from whence we took them. I liked riding so well, that I never was easy but when among the horses; for I used to go to Mr. R___h___d___n, and say, Master, shall I fetch your sheep up out of the field? And if he wanted them, I immediately took the little horse, without saddle or bridle, and mounting on his back, set off as fast as the horse could go, thus running all hazards of my life; and was so wild and heedless, that if any body took notice of my riding so fast, and told me I should fall off, and break my neck, my answer was, "Neck or nothing!" If I happened to fall, I did not care, for I was no sooner off than on again.

I then thought my mother was my greatest enemy; for she being a very passionate woman, used to beat me in such a manner, that the neighbours thought she would kill me. But after my crying was over, I was out of the doors again at my old tricks with my playfellows, and frequently staid out all day long, and never went home at all; for which I was afterwards sure to be corrected.

There was one Mrs. Bax that lived the next door to my mother, who every now-and-then wanted me to bring her something, and often caused me to be beat, so that I did not like her at all. But one morning she asked my mother, to let me fetch her a halfpenny loaf for her breakfast, which my mother ordered me to do. I went to bring the loaf; but thought within myself I would be even with her; and knowing she could not eat the crust, as I came home with it I eat out all the crumb, and putting the two crusts together again, carried it into her house, and laid it down, and then set off for the whole day; for I knew that if I went home I should be beat. When she had found out that I had eat the crumb of the loaf, she told my mother what I had done; but not finding me, my mother told her, that when I came home at night she would chastize me for it, which she accordingly did, and made me go to bed without any supper.

After this, my mother was determined to make me go to service, as soon as she could get a place for me, as she thought I grew worse by running about the streets; and my mistress where I went to school having seven children, the first place I had was with one of her daughters, whose name was Mary Richardson. I staid with her about a year and half, and then returned home to my mother; soon after which I went to school to learn to write.

After I had been at home about a year, I went to live with an elder sister of my former mistress. She was married to one Mr. Goodson, a shoemaker, who was set up in his business, and employed men to work for him. They both lived very happy together; and she had three children by him. But as it pleased God to take my master out of the world, his widow settled herself in a millener's shop, she being capable of making every thing she sold: by this prudent conduct my mistress did very well, and used me kindly, but I was at that time too insensible of the good treatment I met with. She learned me to work with my needle, which if I had but applied myself with proper care and industry, I should, in all probability, have escaped many of the unknown sorrows I afterwards suffered. But, as is commonly the case, when young and unexperienced in the world, we are not aware of the calamities that may befall us as we advance in life. I was so very thoughtless and discontented, that I was always ill, or has some complaint or other to make; but what, I did not know; and would often go and tell my mother my grievances; and, she having a tender heart, believed all I said, and took my part, which contributed to make me idle; and if my mistress said any thing I did not like, though it was for my good, I used to go and represent it in an unfavourable light to my mother; for which behaviour if she had reprimanded or even beat me, I should have left off so childish a practice; and should rather have minded what my mistress said to me, and obeyed her. But being of a roving disposition, I never liked to be within doors; and if I could get out with the young child, I though myself happy; for if I staid within doors, I was idle, and studying what mischief I should do; so that my thoughts were never inclined to any good for myself.

My mistress married a second time to one Mr. Daniel Deverson, a shoemaker, and they lived very happy together; which I might have experienced the good effects of, had I not been of such an untowardly turn of mind; for I had now acquired such a fondness for dancing, that I used to get out of the house in the evening, and be dancing all the night long, which was the beginning of all my sorrow; for by this means I contracted an acquaintance with a new sweetheart, so that I never was contented but when in his company. But happening to be out one night at this pastime, the child cried that used to lie with me, and waked my mistress. She hearing the child cry, called to me, but receiving no answer, got up, and came into my room; but not finding me there, she thought I was gone to a house where a young man used to play on the violin; for she knew the young men and maids met at this house. When my mistress came to the house where I was, she found me very merry and happy; but when I saw her, I was very much surprised, and seemed very sorry for what I had done, because (as it was the first time I was discovered) she thought I had never served her so before; but I had been out time after time, though this was the first occasion of its being known.

The next morning, my mistress told me that I should do myself no good, by going on in this course of life, and gave me some very seasonable advice, if I had been but wise enough to think so; but I took it quite the contrary way, and thought I was not well used; whereupon we agreed to part. I was now about sixteen years of age; and have often since reflected that my mistress bore my misbehaviour and cross temper purely with a view to my advantage, and kept me so long with her for no other purpose, if I could but have thought so; for it is certain she wished me as well as if I had been one of her own children.

After leaving my mistress, I went home, as usual, to my father and mother. I now embraced all opportunities of going out to dance with my sweet heart; for when I was with him I imagined myself happy. But this young man did not perceive that I loved him so much; and it happened very unfortunately I did not tell any of my friends of it; which if I had done, it would probably have been better for me; for my mother would no doubt have persuaded me for my good. But I afterwards felt the bad effects of concealing this warm affection. I could not blame the young man, since he had never given me any reason so to do. Hereupon I was very unsettled in my mind, and unable to fix myself in any place; nevertheless, I carried it off as well as I could.

I had not been long at home, before one Mr. Daniel Stoaders at Ash wanted me to come and live with him; accordingly I went, and liked the place very well; and, had I been but contented, I might have lived there very comfortably. But my mind became continually disturbed and uneasy about this young man, who was the involuntary cause of all my trouble, which was aggravated by my happening to see him one day talk to a young woman: the thoughts of this made me so very unhappy, that I was from that time more unsettled than ever.

A short time after, a thought came into my head to dress myself in mens apparel, and set off by myself; but where to go, I did not know, nor what I was to do when I was gone. I had no thought what was to become of me, or what sorrow and anxiety I should bring upon my aged father and mother by losing me; but my inclinations were still bent on leaving home. In order to do this, I went one day into my master's brother's room, and there found an old frock, an old pair of breeches, an old pair of pumps, and an old pair of stockings, all which did very well; but still was at a great loss for a hat; but then I recollected that my father had got one at home, if I could but procure it unknown to my parents; I therefore intended to get it without their knowledge; whereupon I went to my mother's house to ask her for a gown which I had given her the day before to mend for me. She answered, I should have it to-morrow. But little did my poor mother know what I wanted; for I went immediately into my father's room, took the hat, put it under my apron, and came down stairs; but I never said good-bye, or any thing else to my mother; but went home to my place, and packed up the things that I had got; and now only waited an opportunity to decamp.

On the first day of May, 1759, about six o'clock in the morning, I set off; and when I had got out of town into the fields, I pulled off my cloaths, and put on mens, leaving my own in a hedge, some in one place and some in another. Having thus dressed myself in mens habit, I went on to a place called Wingham, where a fair was held that day. Here I wandered about till evening; then went to a public house, and asked them to let me have a lodging that night, for which I agreed to give two-pence: now all the money I had when I came away was no more than five-pence. Accordingly I went to bed, and slept very well till morning, when I got up, and began to think which way I should go, as my money was so short; however, I proceeded towards Canterbury. But as I was coming along upon the road, a post-chaise overtook me: I got up behind it, and rode to Canterbury; and then the post-chaise stopping, I quitted it, and walked on before, that they might not take any notice of me. After perceiving they did not take the horses out of the chaise, I concluded they were going farther, but did not know where; nor indeed did I care what became of me. When they came on the road to Chatham, I got up behind; not knowing whither I was going, never having been so far from home in my life.

When the chaise had reached Chatham, I got down, but was an utter stranger to the place; only I remembered to have heard my father and mother talk about a man's being hung in chains at Chatham; and, when I saw him, I thought this must be the place. I immediately began to think what I must do for a lodging; having no more than one penny, with which I went and bought some bread and cheese. Here I was quite at a loss what step to take: to go home again, was death to me; and to ask for a lodging, I was ashamed: so I walked up and down the streets, as it was the fair time, and sauntered about till it was dark.

As I stood considering what I should do, I looked about me, and saw a farm-house on the left hand of Chatham, as you go down the hill; I thought within myself I would go to it, and ask them to let me lie there; but when I came down to the house, I was ashamed to make the request. In this distressed situation I continued some time, not knowing how to proceed; for money I had none, and lie in the streets I never was used to, and what to do I did not know: but at last I resolved to lie in the straw, concluding that to be somewhat better than lying in the street; accordingly I went and got in among the straw, and laid myself down, but was so greatly terrified, that I was afraid to move; for when the pigs stirred a little, I thought somebody was coming to frighten me; therefore I did not dare open my eyes, lest I should see something frightful. I had but very little sleep; and when it was morning, I got up and shook my cloaths, and looked about to see if any body perceived me get out. I then came down to the town, and went up to some men that belonged to a collier, who gave me some victuals and drink with them.

While I was standing here, a gentleman came up to me, and asked me if I would go to sea? for, said he, it is fine weather now at sea; and if you will go, I will get you a good master on board the Sandwich. I replied, Yes, Sir. He then shewed me the nearest way on board; but instead of going to St. Princess's-bridge, (as the gentleman had directed me) I went over where the tide came up, being half up my legs in mud; but at length I got up to the bridge, and seeing a boat there, I asked the men belonging to it, if they were going on board the Sandwich? They told me they were; and asked me if I wanted to go on board? I told them, Yes. They enquired who I wanted there? I told them, The gunner. They laughed, said I was a brave boy, and that I would do very well for him. But I did not know who was to be my master, or what I was to do, or whether I had strength to perform it: They then carried me on board.

When I came along-side the Sandwich, there were lighters with rigging or something belonging to her: that appeared all strange to me, as I never had seen such a large ship before; having often seen the hoys at Sandwich haven. When getting out of the lighter into the Sandwich, I thought it was impossible for such a great ship to go to sea. But what the men most took notice of, was, my observing how many windows the ship had got; she not yet having got her guns on board, for her ports were open.

When I found that the men laughed at me, I was angry with myself, for saying any thing before I was acquainted with it. The sailors asked me if I would go to the gunner, who was in his cabbin in the gun-room. Accordingly I went down: but it was remarkable I did not then know the head of the ship from the stern; for when I was down I could not find the way up again. When the gunner saw me, he asked where I came from, and how I came there? I told him, I had left my friends. He enquired if I had been 'prentice to any body, and run away? I told him, No. Well, said he, should you like to go to sea? I replied, Yes, Sir. He then asked if I was hungry? I answered in the affirmative; having had but very little all the day. Upon this, he ordered his servant to serve me some biscuit and cheese. The boy went and brought me some, and said, Here countryman, eat heartily; which I accordingly did: for the biscuit being new, I liked it well, or else my being hungry made it go down very sweet and savoury. After I had eat sufficiently, the gunner came and asked my name. I told him my name was WILLIAM CHANDLER: but God knows how that came into my head; though it is true, my mother's maiden name was Chandler, and my father's name William Lacy; therefore I took the name of Chandler. Then the gunner told his boy to give me some victuals with him; and that when he went on shore, I was to go with him, (Jeremiah Pane, for that was his name) and we agreed very well: for he used to carry the people over the river, which sometimes put a few pence in his pocket; so that he always had some money, and was very good to me, and often gave me some, with which we sometimes tossed up for pies: therefore I lived very happy, considering the condition and situation I was in at that time.

There was another circumstance that attended me; for though I could not play the rogue much at first, yet in a little time afterwards I learned to do it very completely. But not knowing all this time who was my master, made me dissatisfied; for I had no linen to clean myself with, having only the shift that I had when I came from Ash; and I was very much afraid my fellow-servant should see my shirt had no collar; and besides, I had no other cloaths to wear but those I had on, which gave me such concern, that I often wished I was at home again. But the thoughts of seeing the young man again when I went home, diverted me entirely from that resolution, and made me conclude, that I had rather live upon bread and water, and go through all the trouble that I had brought, or might hereafter bring upon myself, than go home again.

I had been on board the Sandwich about four days when the carpenter came on board; and he had only one servant, who was at work in Chatham Yard; so at that time he had none on board. Now the gunner, whose name was

Rd. Ruffel, liked me very well: he lived in lodgings at a place called Brompton, near Chatham; and the land-lady of the house where he lodged had a son, who wanted to go to sea; and this woman was willing, if the gunner would take him, that he should go: whereupon the gunner and she agreed that he should go to sea with him as his servant. He told me, the carpenter would be glad to have me as his servant, for he was not willing I should be the captain's servant, that being the worst place in the ship, but at that time I did not know which was the best or worst: Mr. Ruffel, the gunner, therefore spoke to Mr. Richard Baker, the carpenter, for me. I was then sent for to the carpenter's cabbin. He asked me, Whether I had been an apprentice to any body, and was run away? I told him, No. Well, said he, are you a Kentish boy, or a boy of Kent? For my part, I did not then know the difference between a Kentish boy and a boy of Kent; but I answered, A boy of Kent, which happened to be right. This made him laugh at me; for he was a merry man; but when out of humour, it was trouble enough to please him.

I shall here take occasion to relate what my master said to me concerning being his servant. There were two gentlemen with him. He first of all ordered me to fetch him a can of beer: I accordingly went, and brought it to him. Now, said he, you must learn to make a can of flip, and to broil me a beef steak, and to make my bed against I come to live on board. Come, said he, and I will show you how to make my bed. So we went to his cabbin, in which there was a bed that turned up, and he began to take the bed cloaths off one by one. Now, said he, you must shake them one by one, you must tumble and shake the bed about, then you must lay the sheets on one at a time, and lastly the blankets. I replied, Yes, Sir. Well, said he, you will soon learn to make a bed, that I see already. But he little knew who he had got to make his bed; and he not having any suspicion of my being a woman, I affected to appear as ignorant of the matter as if I had known nothing about it. He then provided for me a bed and bedding of a boatswain who came on board to see him, and then directed his mate to sling it up for me. When I attempted to get into bed at night, I got in at one side, and fell out on the other, which made all the seamen laugh at me; but, at it happened, there were not a great many on board, for being a new ship, but few had entered on board of her; so that my hammock was hung up in the sun-deck: but when the whole ship's company was on board, it was then taken down, and placed below in the wing where the carpenter and the yeomen both were; now it was better for me to lay there than anywhere else. But I was very uneasy by lying there, on account of a quarter-master that lay in that place, whom I did not much like: and when I came to lie in the blankets, I did not know what to do, for I thought I was eat up with vermin, having been on board ten days, and had no cloaths to shift myself with; so that I looked black enough to frighten any body.

One day my master came on board, which was on a Saturday, and called me to go along with him; he had me up on the gangway, and shewed me three hay stacks, and asked me if I saw them. I told him, Yes, Sir. Well, said he, I would have you come on shore to-morrow morning, in the first boat that you can get: walk till you have lost sight of those hay stacks, and then enquire for one Mr. Baker, at St. Margaret's Bank, Chatham; and when you come to my house, you shall clean yourself: after which, my master went on shore; and I immediately thought that I had a great many particulars to remember; for fear therefore I should forget them, (as I could write well enough for myself to understand) I went to my pantry door, and there I set it down. When the morning was come, I got up, and took the direction off the door, set it down on my hat, got on shore as soon as I could, and made all possible haste to find out my master's house, and walked till I had lost sight of the hay stacks. Seeing a woman stand at the door, I asked her where one Mr. Baker, carpenter of the Sandwich lived? She shewed me the house: and when I was got there, how glad was I! For I longed to see my mistress, and what sort of a house they lived in. I went and knocked, and there came a woman to the door, of whom I enquired, if one Mr. Baker lived there? Whereupon she fell a laughing, and said, What do you want with him? I told her, my master had ordered me to come to him. Then she laughed again, and asked me if I knew my master when I saw him? I answered, Yes. She then bid me come in. I went into the kitchen where my master was sitting. My mistress asked me if that was my master? I replied Yes, ma'am. My master next enquired if I was hungry? Indeed I thought I could gladly eat a bit of bread and butter, and drink a bason of tea, for I even longed for some, having had none since I came away from Ash. But I told him, I was not hungry; notwithstanding which, he being a merry man, said to me, You can eat a little bit? I answered, Yes, Sir. On my saying this, my mistress gave me a bason of tea, and a bit of bread and butter, more than I could eat; but I quickly found out a way to dispose of the remainder, for what I could not eat, I put in my pocket.

When I had eaten my breakfast, my master called me out backwards, where there was some soap and water to wash myself with. How glad was I! Hardly being able to contain myself for joy. But there was something that gave me greater pleasure; for after I had washed myself, my mistress gave me a clean shirt, a pair of stockings, a pair of shoes, a coat and waistcoat, a checked handkerchief, and a red night-cap for me to wear at sea: I was also to have my hair cut off when I went on board; but this operation I did not like at all, yet was afraid to say any thing to my master about it. However, I was very glad to find I had got clean cloaths to dress myself in, not having had that refreshment since I left Ash.

I must next inform you what trouble I was in; for I was afraid that my master would want to see my shirt; but my fears were soon over; for he only ordered me to put up all my cloaths together, and carry them on board with me. Now if I had changed my linen at his house, he would have seen my shift, and then he would have easily discovered my sex. Accordingly I took my things, went on board, and cleaned myself from top to toe. My master told me that I must wash my things every Monday, and that he would look them over every week; and, said he, if I don't find them clean, I shall flog you. Still I was in great trouble, lest he should ask me for my white shirt, for I had never a one to screen me from telling a lie; but I knew that Jeremiah Pane had got one; so I went and asked him if he would sell me his shirt; for it was not worth a great deal. Well, said he, you shall have it for nine-pence. I replied, I will give you nine-pence for it. He agreed; I paid him the money, and got the shirt, to my no small joy. I then went and washed it, and carried it to my locker, for fear my master should ask me about it.

The ship had now orders to sail to Black Stakes, to take in her guns; consequently we proceeded to get them in. When I came to see the guns, I thought it was impossible for the ship to carry them, they being so large; for I had never seen a man-of-war before; so that it seemed very strange to me. But we had not lain long at Black Stakes before we went to the Nore, and there we lay till farther orders. We had now got a great number of men on board; some we had from the Polly Green, some from one ship, and some from another. These men were paid off from their several ships to come on board with us. But while we lay at the Nore, there came a bomb boat woman on board us, to sell all sorts of goods; this woman being an acquaintance of my master's, she had the use of his cabbin; therefore I was desired to boil the tea kettle for her, and to do any thing she ordered me; and I was glad of it, for she was very good to me, and gave me a new purse to put my money in. Now my master kept the key of the round-house; therefore the women had no convenient place of easing the necessity of nature; and he told me not to let them have the key, unless they gave me something; by this means I got several pence from them. My master then told me that my mistress was coming on board, and intended to stay all night, and desired me not to go from the cabbin door, lest she should want me. Agreeable to my instructions, I sat down by the cabbin door, and ran and fetched every thing that she had occasion for, but when I carried her any thing, instead of pulling off my hat, I was ready to make a curtsy, however, they did not take any notice of me. In general, I pleased her very well, never having any disagreement with one another.

It being now the last time that my mistress was to be on board, my master asked permission to go on shore, to take leave of all his friends and acquaintance; for we did not know how soon we might sail; and when we were out at sea, none of us knew that we might live to return again. My master and mistress therefore went on shore, and determined to take me with them; and I was very proud to think that I was to go with them to Chatham. We went all on shore, and had a supper dressed at the sign of the Sun: and when we broke up, my master and mistress went home, and I went along with them, and lay at their house. In the morning, I got up, eat my breakfast, and did what my mistress desired me: after she had breakfasted, we went and bought two check shirts and a pair of shoes for me to carry to sea, which occasioned me to think that I was well furnished, as I had four shirts and other necessities;

therefore I thought that I was a sailor every inch of me. When my mistress and I came home, we shewed my master what we had bought; he told me I should have a box made to put my cloaths in, and gave me a strict charge to take care of them; for he said, when I came on board, they would steal the teeth out of my head if they could. I promised I would be as careful as possible of them. Well, said he, I hope you will; then told me we must go on board that evening; and added, I shall look at your cloaths, to see how clean you have kept them; which last expression gave me a great deal of uneasiness, through fear of a discovery. My master and mistress parted after this, and we went on board; for we could not tell how soon the ship might sail.

After I was got on board, I began to think where I was going; for neither my father or mother knew where I was all this while, nor what was become of me; therefore my thoughts began to trouble me exceedingly, as I did not know whether I should live to come home again, or should ever see my disconsolate father and mother any more. These considerations occasioned me to reflect what sorrow and grief I had brought on my aged parents, who no doubt were very unhappy in having lost me so long. But seeing I had brought this misfortune on myself, I formed a resolution to go through with it, and suffer the consequences: for my mind suggested to me, that when I was out at sea, I could not run away; and if they discovered that I was a woman, I concluded it would be utterly impossible for me to escape. The serious reflection of these circumstances so aggravated the disquietude of my mind, that I did not know what to do: but I was the sole cause of all this perplexity myself.

I shall here take an opportunity of advising all maidens, never to give their minds to frequent the company of young men, or to seem fond of them: and I would also caution them, not to addict themselves to dancing with the male sex, as I wantonly did. But had I been in bed and asleep, which I ought to have been, the unknown sorrows I have since felt and experienced, would not have befallen me: but then I was young and foolish, and had not the thought or care of an older person. I would likewise admonish all young men, to beware how they marry; for I have seen so much of my own sex, that it is enough for a man to hate them; however, there are good and bad of both sexes.

I shall now proceed to relate some farther instances of my folly. In the first place, I thought, were I at home, I should be very happy if I could only see the young man again that I came away for; but a little recollection convinced me, it was in vain to think about that, as I could not run away; so by degrees this notion wore off, and I became quite contented: but when my master spoke angry, I used to sit down and cry for hours together. One day he told me I must go on shore with him at Sheerness, and take the little hand-basket with me, to bring spinach on board: so we went on shore, and the wind blew fresh. We did not stay long, but soon came on board again; which I was very desirous of, it being more agreeable to me to be on board than elsewhere.

After this, my master began to teach me the nature of the ship, and how to cook for him, which gave me an opportunity of discovering his natural temper. Sometimes, on mere trifling occasions, he was very hot, when things were not done according to his mind; on that account I was always afraid of him, and generally (when he was in a passion) stood with the cabbin door in my hand, in order to make escape; which when I did, he always beat me. This usage I could hardly brook, especially as I knew that I was as real a woman as his mother. Besides, when at home, I could not bear to be spoke to, much less to have my faults told me. But now I found it was come to blows; and thought it was very hard to be struck by a man; which occasioned me to reflect that there was a wide difference between being at home, and in my present situation abroad.

About this time, orders came for us to sail immediately, to join the fleet at Brest, which put me under the most terrible apprehensions of coming to anchor in the Downs, lest I should see somebody there that knew me, being so near home. But it happened according to my wishes, since we did not anchor there; for having a fair wind, we sailed through the channel, and soon found the ship was too light for want of ballast. However, we quickly joined the fleet at Brest, and the captain of the Sandwich, with admiral Geary, came on board us, and took the command of her, who hoisted his flag at the mizzen. With the admiral, came all his followers, both men and boys; and our hands were all turned over to the Resolution. We had now our full complement, which was 100. But among the admiral's servants, there were a great number of stout boys, very wicked and mischievous, and quite different in temper and behaviour from those of ours, who were sent from the Marine Society by Justice Fielding. I never was under the least apprehension of these marine boys offering to molest or fight me; but those sturdy boys belonging to the admiral, were every now and then trying to pick a quarrel with me, nor was it long before they found means to put their design in execution; for one day being sent down in the galley to broil a beef steak, one of these audacious boys, whose name was William Severy, came and gave me such a slap in the face, that made me reel. This insult brought a little choler on me, which by repeated affronts almost grew into fury. I

considered it would only make me sick if I could not beat
him; and also reflected that my cause was just, for I never
had attempted to anger him, though he was perpetually
using me ill. From these considerations, on his next abuse,
I was determined to try the event. Lieutenant Cook
knowing me better than any of them, and at the same time
being sensible that I had given no just cause for these pro-
ceedings, told me I should fight him, and if conqueror,
should have a plum pudding, and that he would in the
mean time mind the steak. Upon which, I went aft to
the main hatchway, and pulled off my jacket; but they
wanted me to pull off my shirt, which I would not suffer,
for fear of being discovered that I was a woman, and it
was with much difficulty that I could keep it on. Hereupon
we instantly engaged, and fought a great while; but, during
the combat, he threw me such violent cross buttocks, that
were almost enough to dash my brains out; but I never
gave out, for I knew if I did, I should have one or other of
them continually upon me: therefore we kept to it with
great obstinacy on both sides; and I soon began to get
the advantage of my antagonist, which all the people
who knew me perceiving, seemed greatly pleased, especially when he declined fighting any more; and the more
so, as he was looked upon as the best fighter among
them.

This contest ending so favourably for me, I reigned master over the rest, they being all afraid of me: and it was a most lucky circumstance, that I had spirit and vigour to conquer him who was my greatest adversary; for if I had not, I should have been so harassed and ill-treated amongst them, that my very life would have been a burden. However, all the time I was fighting, my master knew nothing of the matter; but, when over, somebody told him. As soon as I had put myself in some tolerable order, I went for the steak, and carried it to his cabbin, being a little afraid that I should be chastized. Well, said he, you have been a long while about the steak, I hope it is well done now? Yes, Sir, said I. Why, says he, looking very attentively, I suppose you have been fighting? I answered, Yes, Sir, I was forced to fight, or else be drubbed. But, said he, I hope you have not been beat? I replied, No, Sir. Well, said he, when you fight again, let me know, and I will be bound you shall beat them; so that, upon the whole, I came off with flying colours. From this time, the boy and I who fought, became as well reconciled to one another as if we had been brothers; and he always let me share part of what he had.

It was now more than two months since I had left my father and mother, who had never heard of me; about which time, we received orders for the Resolution to sail for England, to be repaired. I observed the people now on board were employing themselves in writing letters to their friends; which put a thought into my head to write to my mother, to inform her where I was, which I knew would be a great satisfaction to my parents. I could write but very indifferently; and to entrust any person with my thoughts on this occasion, I imagined would be very improper. At last, I resolved to write myself; but, after having wrote my letter, I had nothing to seal it with, and, thinking a bit of pitch would do, I went to the pitch-tub for some, which when I thought I had got, it proved to be tar, so that with using it I soiled the letter very much. I was now greatly perplexed to contrive a method to seal it up. At length, one of the men, who observed I had been writing, gave me a wafer, which did completely. Soon after this, the boat came on board, and took away all the letters, and mine with the rest; the contents of which I now present you with, and are as follows:

"*Hond. Father and Mother,*   *July 3, 1759.*

"*This comes with my duty to you, and hope that you are both in good health, as I am at present, thanks be to God for it. I would have you make yourselves as easy as you can, for I have got a very good master, who is carpenter on board the Sandwich; and am now upon the French coast, right over Brest: shall be glad to hear from you as soon as you can. So no more at present, from*

"Your undutiful Daughter,
"MARY LACY.

P.S. Please to direct thus, For William Chandler, on board the Sandwich, at Brest".

These were the contents of the Letter I sent to my father and mother, to acquaint them where I was; and give occasion to the reflection, that children too often grieve and distress their parents by rash and disobedient behaviour; and many, alas! bring sorrow and trouble upon their heads, at the very period of life it behoves them rather to add to their comfort and joy, by all the means in their power.

In about six weeks after, while we lay at Brest, I received a Letter from my father and mother. When the men called and told me there was a Letter for me, I immediately ran for joy to think that I got an answer sent me; but, nevertheless, was afraid to open it, lest I should find therein a severe rebuke for running away; however, at last, (with some reluctance) I broke it open, and, to my great pleasure and satisfaction, found it contained as follows:

"My dear Child, Ash,　　　　　　*Aug. 16, 1759.*

I received your's safe, and was glad to hear that you are in good health; but I have been at death's door almost with grief for you. Your cloaths, after your departure, were found in a hedge, which occasioned me to think you were murdered; therefore I have had no rest day or night; for I thought, that if you had been alive, you would have writ to me before. However, as you have writ to me now, I shall make myself as easy as I can; but shall still have hopes of seeing you again. And I hope you will put your trust in God, and beg that he will help you in all your difficulties and trials. When you have an opportunity to write to me, don't be neglectful; and may the blessing of God be with you! So no more at present, from

"Your afflicted Father and Mother,
"WM. and MARY LACY."

After I had read the letter, I could not help crying, to think what trouble and sorrow I had brought on my parents; and on considering that I should be the cause of bringing aged hairs with sorrow to the grave, perhaps much sooner than might otherwise have happened. I must therefore here address myself to all undutiful children, hoping they will mind what I say, and be attentive to the instructions and advice of their parents in their youthful days, whereby they may escape many dangers and miseries that a forward and stubborn conduct will bring upon them.

Whilst I was reading my letter, one of the boys went and told my master that I was crying; on his observing which, he asked me what I cried for, and if any body had abused me? I answered, No, Sir. What is the cause then, said he? I beg you will tell me. I then gave him to understand I had received a Letter from my father and mother. Well, said he, are they dead or alive? I told him, they were alive and well; but that I was afraid they would chide me for running away. He observed, I like you the better for remembering your parents; and God will love all them who love their parents. On hearing him express himself thus, I thought God was very merciful to me, in directing me to such a good master: for if he beat me himself, he would not suffer any body else to do so: besides, I knew his temper so well, that nobody else could please him like myself, which indeed I sometimes found it very difficult to do; for if any thing went contrary to his mind, and made him angry, he would be sure to vent it on somebody or other. Upon the whole, it was a hard matter to please him; for he would on some occasions fall into such violent passions, that he neither knew what he said or did. He frequently accustomed himself to sit up late, either with the gunner or boatswain; who, when they all met together, would continue in each other's company during the whole night, which obliged me to be up very late on my master's account; and have frequently been kept so long from my rest till I have been stiff and almost dead with cold. When in liquor, he used to make me many fair promises; and, amongst others, that he would put me 'prentice, and find me with all my cloaths during the time; and that I should have my money to send home to my parents. After talking to me in this manner, he would add, William, you are a good boy; and though I scold you sometimes, it is only because you don't do as I desire you: however, you are a good boy in the main, too. I must also tell you, William, that your mistress is a very good woman: but, do you hear me? Don't tell her that I say so, or that I sit up late at night. She will ask you a great many questions about me, and what company I keep, but be sure not to inform her.

It may not be improper to observe here, that of all the officers boys in the ship, the boatswain's was the least serviceable of any, inasmuch as he could not even boil the kettle for his master's breakfast; so that I used to do that and other things for him. The boatswain, I must own, was very good to me for it; as he gave me a pair of stockings, and several other necessaries, which made me take delight to wait on him: and my master told me, that I might go to his cabbin when I pleased. But this good fortune did not last long; for, he being ordered away from our ship, I lost a good friend; after which, I had reason to apply the proverb to my own case, which says, "When the old one is gone, there seldom comes a better;" as he was, through his obliging behaviour, beloved by the whole ship's company. He was succeeded by a boatswain taken from the Somerset man-of-war.

A few days after, as gunner and boatswain's boy were sitting down to dinner, and myself standing (being always in a hurry, and indifferent whether I stood or sat) my master observing from his cabbin that the boatswain's boy was sitting while I was standing near him, immediately ordered me to make him rise, and take his seat. For my part, I did not desire to do any such thing, as I imagined it would have been looked upon as a very great breach of good manners to disturb any person so roughly.

Another time the lieutenant told me to put a hand to the staysail braces, and help to hale them up. My master seeing this, called to me, and asked what I was doing? I told him the lieutenant ordered me to do it. He replied, You have no business to do any such work; nor, added he, shall a servant of mine do any thing of that nature; and cautioned me to remember, that I did not come to be their servant, but his.

As we lay still at Brest, some men were draughted from the Temple to come on board us: amongst them was a young man that I knew at Ash, whose name was Henry Hambrook; and I was much afraid he would know me. However, having been on board for some time, he one day came and asked, if I did not come from Ash? Not being willing to know him, I enquired what reason he had for asking such a question? O, said he, I thought I knew you. However, I took no farther notice of what he said concerning me: nor did he mention the matter again to any other person, to my knowledge, though he well knew who I was.

Soon after this, I was taken with the rheumatism in my fingers, which occasioned them to swell very much: not knowing the cause, I went and shewed them to my master. Let me see your fingers, said he, and fell a laughing at me, adding, hang me if William is not growing rich: You dog, you have got the gout in your fingers. This passed on a day or two, when I was seized with it in my legs, and was so bad that I could not walk. My master was then at a loss what to do with me; but thought proper to send down for the doctor to come and look at me. He told me, that I must go down into the bay in the sick birth. Well knowing what a nasty unwholesome place it was, the very thoughts of going thither made me very uneasy; nevertheless, I did not choose to say any thing to my master about it. I was accordingly carried down; but he sent me thither every day some tea and biscuit buttered for breakfast. This I received from the hands of an old man, who was of so uncleanly a disposition, that had I been ever so well, I could not have relished it from him. I remained in this disagreeable place for several weeks; but, growing worse and worse, was much altered.

While in this disagreeable situation, the young man above-mentioned frequently came down to see me; but never took any notice that he knew me. Thinking therefore, that he came out of friendship, I desired him to tell my master that I should be glad he would move me to some other part of the ship, for if he did not, it would soon be the death of me. He immediately went and related all I had said to him. Whereupon my master came down to see me; when I told him as before, that I should soon die if not removed from thence. Well, said he, you shall come up and sit in my cabbin. And indeed very glad I was to think I should be taken out of that loathsome place. He then sent two men to bring me into his cabbin, and ordered the yeoman to warm some water to wash my hands and face, which he cleaned and wiped himself; and took as much care of me as if I had been one of this own, which he evidenced by many instances of his goodness towards me.

I was unable to sit up in the cabbin the whole day, and at night was carried down. Next morning, when the doctor called to visit the sick, he asked me how I did? I answered, Very bad. He then began to be very angry that I went up to my master's cabbin and told me, I should not go there any more till I was better. Upon which, I fell a crying, which I could not help, on thinking I must be confined below. In order to prevent, if possible, this disagreeable circumstance, I desired the man to acquaint my master what the doctor had said. In consequence of which, my master went down to the doctor, and told him roundly, that I should come up every day to his cabbin, for my staying there was the readiest way to kill me. Accordingly I was allowed to come up every day as before; by which means I soon became better. But being still very weak, my master got me crutches, with a spike at each end, for my safety to walk about on the deck; and, when any body affronted me in an ill-natured way, I used to throw my crutch at them. The care I was constantly taken of by the person under whom Providence had placed me was such, that he would not suffer me to wait on him, lest I should catch cold again; so that by this precaution I soon recovered my health and strength.

In a short time after, we received orders to sail to Plymouth, to take in ballast and more provision, and afterwards to join the fleet again at Brest. When we were returned, admiral Hawke made a signal for all the fleet to clear ship, which we did for three or four days; expecting the French fleet out every hour. But finding they made no preparation to leave the harbour, we put up all the officers cabbins; and, on the 10th of November 1759, being his majesty's birthday, the admiral made a signal for all the ships to fire the same number of guns as in England on this occasion. We ran in as near the French coast as we could; after which, the admiral began to fire: and after having fired all round, we all tack'd about, and stood off from the land; yet did not stand far off, but lay to, to see if the enemy would venture out. It seemed as if they thought we were going to land at Brest, or some other place; for in the night they made bonfires all round the country, to alarm and give notice to their people, that we were about to land. But when the wind was fair for us to stand off from the shore, it was favourable for them to sail. Soon after, it blowing hard, and from a proper point for us to quit the French coast, the admiral made a signal for all the fleet to anchor in Torbay; which we accordingly did.

During the time the Sandwich lay in the foresaid bay, orders came for us to sail to Plymouth. But while we were under way, there came a ship acquainting the admiral that the French fleet had got out, and were directing their course towards the West Indies. Immediately upon this intelligence, some of our ships cut their cables, others weighed their anchors, and we soon came up with them at Quiberon-bay, where we began the engagement, and soon forced them to surrender; for some sheered off, others were taken, and several of them threw their guns overboard: So after dispersing and destroying the best fleet they had, we imagined the war would soon be at an end. However, our ship had no share in the battle, for we were at that time in Plymouth; but soon received orders to go to Quiberon bay, to watch the motions of the French there. Hereupon we sailed, and anchored in the bay; and had a great deal of pleasure in viewing the country, as we were stationed there some time.

My master now asked me how I liked the sea? I replied, I liked it very well. But, said he, should you not be afraid if you were to come to an engagement? I answered, No; for I should have work enough to fetch powder to the gun I was quartered at, therefore should have no time to think of that. He then told me, I should not be able to bring the powder fast enough. I replied, I'll take it from the little boys, and cause them to fetch more, before the gun shall want powder; at which he laughed heartily, to hear me talk so, as he well might.

We continued here for some time; and were afterwards ordered to the Bay of Biscay. I must here observe, that a person, who is a stranger to these great and boisterous seas, would think it impossible for a large ship to ride in them: but I slept many months on the ocean, where I have been tossed up and down at an amazing rate. As we were stationed off Cape Finisterre, and the wind blowing so hard that we could not lie there, we afterwards went and anchored in Quiberon bay, and when there, the officers went frequently on shore; which our master perceiving, obtained leave for me to go with the admiral's boys when an opportunity offered.

About this time, the princess' boat went on shore, accompanied by all the band of music; and we had a great deal of pleasure in walking about the island in the day time; but there were very few people in it. When they saw our boat coming on shore, they sent the young women out of the island, for fear of our officers; and there were left remaining only two or three old men, and one old woman. We here found very fine grapes, and other sort of fruits; but our officers would not allow us to take any of their fruits, except grapes; and if we had an inclination for any others, we were obliged to pay for them. I saw no other habitations than two or three old huts which they lived in.

In the evening we went on board; when my master asked me how I liked the island? I told him, I liked it very well, and that I thought it was a very pleasant place; but imagined it must be extremely cold in winter. Notwithstanding this agreeableness of his temper at intervals, it was in general a difficult matter to please him; for sometimes, after providing one thing for his breakfast, he would require another; for instance, when I had made sage tea, he would have gruel; and, after green, he would order bohea to be made, with biscuit split, toasted and buttered; and if either of these things were prepared in any respect displeasing to him, he would fling it at me, though not with any real intention of hurting me; nay, the very cups and saucers would not escape his violent passion: so that I was afraid of getting ready his breakfast lest he should flog me, and then I should run the utmost risk of being discovered. On this account I was always upon my guard as much as possible. One time when I did not get his breakfast to please him, he told me I should be flogged at the gun for my neglect; and being afraid he would do it, I sat down and cried all the time the gunner and he were at breakfast. My master afterwards said to the gunner, Don't you think now that William ought to be flogged for not getting the breakfast better? But the gunner being always a good friend to me, said, I will be bound for William this time that he will do so no more. What! returned my master, will you, who have been bound so often for him, be answerable again for his good behaviour? If so, for this time I'll take your word; but remember, the next time he does any thing amiss, I will send for you, and then you shall be flogged for him. By this means I got off scot free. He would sometimes kick me with such violence, as if he would force me through the cabbin; and when he had the gout, would be so peevish and passionate, that I found it extremely troublesome and difficult to please him, insomuch that I often wished him dead.

My master once told me, he should come and look in my locker again, to see what things I had there. Accordingly he came; and on examining it, he missed the blacking bottle, in which I used to make his blacking. Knowing it was broke, I stood off for fear, as I knew I should expose myself to his resentment. He asked me, Where is the blacking bottle? I answered, Sir, it is broke. He then fell into a great passion. You dog, said he, I will have you flogged for it; I thought my shoes did not shine as they used to do. However, I happily escaped the flogging at this time. He always caused me clean my own shoes as well as those that belonged to him; and if they were not done to his mind, he would kick me with great violence. Whereupon he peremptorily expressed himself thus, You dog, I will make you go neat and clean; for you are a carpenter's servant, and you shall appear as such.

Not long after this circumstance, my master was seized with another severe fit of the gout, which increased to such a degree, that I was obliged to sew some flannel upon his legs; and if I did not do it to please him, I was sure to be severely reprimanded; and he was withal so troublesome, that if I was but just lain down in my hammock, he would send somebody to fetch me up; therefore I had but little rest at a time, as he was always wanting something. If I was gone only a minute from the cabbin door, he would pass the word fore and aft for boy William, as he called me; so that I was forced to run, lest I should be chastized. But when every thing went agreeable with him, he would then be apt to make me many fair promises; and, among others, that he would bind me out 'prentice, and clothe me during the time, though I could never believe it would come to any thing.

At this time, there were the Ramillies, the Royal William, and five other ships with us; but on January 12,

1760, a dreadful hurricane arose, which lasted two days; by reason of this storm we lost sight of each other, not knowing where we were; and the sea running mountains high, all of us expected to perish. We had seven men drowned, had sprung our main and foremast, and were very nigh the land; but as it pleased God to give us a sight of the danger we were in, we very happily kept clear of the land, and next day went into Plymouth Sound, when my master went on shore into the yard to report the damage of the ship. I went with him; and we were greatly affected on seeing that only twenty-five men were saved out of 700 that were in the Ramillies, which was lost on the 14th of January, 1760. On this melancholy occasion, I thought God was very good and merciful to us, that we escaped in that terrible tempest; notwithstanding which, we were no sooner delivered from the danger of the seas than we forgot it, and neglected to give God thanks for so great a mercy; but on the contrary, were still from one day to another running on in a greater course of wickedness than before.

I now thought that if I could but get clear of the ship, I should esteem myself very happy, but recollected I had no money; for my master had never paid me any; and my cloaths were made out of old canvas. When I was served with wine, I sold it for two shillings a bottle, and that helped to provide me some shirts; for I had very little money of my master.

At this time we received orders to go into the Hamoaze, to have our ship repaired, which I was glad of, as I always went on shore with my master, who frequented the sign of the Cross Keys at North Conner, kept by one Mr. P____s. He obtained leave to stay on shore, and gave me the like permission till he went on board. An unfortunate circumstance attended me here, which was, that I had a bedfellow allotted me, being obliged to lie with the post-chaise boy, which gave me great concern; however, it was the will of God I should not be discovered at that time, though I continued in this situation while the ship lay at Plymouth.

When my master was sober, he would sit down and reckon what money he had spent, the thoughts of which ruffled his temper greatly, and at such times I was always the chief object of his resentment; therefore I was sorry when he was not in liquor.

In a short time our ship was ready to go to sea again; then my master and the gunner went into the country to buy some fowls, pigs, ducks, and a great quantity of garden stuff, which were all carried on board. Being ready for sea, we were ordered to proceed to Rochelle and Basque Roads, and keep our station there till further orders. We had not been long at sea before my master was seized with such a severe fit of gout, that I thought he would have died before we could get home; therefore I heartily wished we were in England again. Besides, I had no peace day after day; and as he still grew worse and worse, I was quite tired of my life, having a great number of different kinds of messes continually to make for him.

One day as he was sitting in his cabbin, he told me he heard we were going for England; and he seemed greatly pleased, as well as I, that the ship had received orders to sail for Portsmouth; because I thought he would then have liberty to go into sick quarters as soon as he could. When we came in sight of the Isle of Wight, my master began to pack up all his things to be ready to go on shore at Portsmouth; and on his arrival there, he wrote a letter to Chatham for my mistress to come down to him. It was not long before she came on board the Sandwich, where she lay all night, but was soon tired of the ship. Next day my mistress was conducted all over the cabbin, when she asked my master several trivial questions concerning the time how long he had had this and the other convenience. To all which, he told her, it was as *his master* pleased; for when he was in a good humour he would call me so. She did not find fault with any thing, but was soon tired of being on board, which I was not sorry for, because I thought I should then have a little time to myself.

My master having liberty to go on shore, took lodgings at one Mr. Allen's, a shipwright, where I accompanied him; and as a favourable opportunity offered itself, by the leisure time afforded me here, I resolved to embrace it, in order to write to my parents, which I did in the following terms:

Portsmouth, Oct. 27, 1760

"Hond. Father and Mother,

This comes with my duty to you, and hope these lines will find you in good health, as I am at present. I am very sorry that I ran away from you, and that I have been so neglectful in writing; but I beg leave to tell you, that I have no thoughts of coming to Ash again, but should be very glad to see you; however, in that I must trust to the will of God. Last January, in a storm of wind, we lost seven men. The Ramillies was lost at the same time, and only 25 men saved; but by the blessing of God it was not my lot. I am in some hopes I shall have a little money to send you, when my master pays me; for

I have received none yet. He talks of paying soon; so that you need not expect to hear from me till such time as I am able to send you what money I can spare. My kind love to my brother and sister, and all friends that know me. Shall be glad to hear from you as soon as you can conveniently write. So no more at present, from

    "Your undutiful Daughter,
    "MARY LACY.

N.B. Please to direct thus, For William Chandler, on board the Sandwich, in Portsmouth harbour.

I shall now return to my master and mistress. Being on shore, one day he told me I must go on board with him next morning. We staid in the ship that night; and in the morning he packed up some wine for me to carry on shore: But the wind blowing fresh, he would go in a cutter that was there; and not being able to reach the harbour, we were obliged to land at the south beach. Just upon our reaching the shore the cutter filled with water, which made us very wet; and from this unfortunate accident, I had the basket of wine to carry full two miles to Portsmouth Common, after having narrowly escaped with our lives. However, we got home in good time, though I was obliged to lie at a public house, the sign of the Ship and Castle.

In the morning I went down to my master's lodgings, and did the usual business; such as cleaning his room, and getting his breakfast ready. My mistress then began to enquire in what condition my cloaths were, and whether they wanted repair? My master told her, he had bought me a purser's jacket, but it was too big. Whereupon she ordered me to bring my things on shore when I went on board again, and she would teach me how to mend them. Accordingly I went on board, and brought them with me: and my mistress and I being alone, she began to ask how my master and I agreed? What time he went to bed, and what company he kept? I told her, the gunner and he, who both messed together, were very agreeable; that my master kept very regular hours, and went to bed in good time: for I took great care not to say any thing that might cause a disagreement betwixt them. Nevertheless, she would often shift me from one thing to another; yet I still kept upon my guard: And telling her at last I knew nothing of the things she questioned me about, she left off importuning me.

Next day my mistress told me I must to the town-market with her, to buy something for Sunday's dinner.

Taking the hand-basket with me, we went together; but had not gone far before we met with one or two of the sailors companions who knew me. They asked me how I did; and a little conversation passed betwixt us. My mistress did not stop to observe who they were, or what they said: but when I came up to her again, she asked me who they were? I told her what I knew of them. When we came to the market, my mistress was always upon the wing, going from one place to another, asking the price of several things, and at length she bought of those whose provisions she cheapened at first; and after having bought a duck, we went home to our lodgings.

As soon as my master came home, his wife began to tell him how many women had been enquiring after me. Well, said my master, I suppose you have boiled the tea kettle for them? Yes, Sir, said I, I have, for I don't like to be ill-natured; if I had, I should have been beat very unmercifully ere now; but thank God I never had the ill will of any of them; and I believe if any of them had seen me ill used, they would have taken my part. My master replied, I would have you learn to be good natured to every body, and not to practice any bad tricks.

I still continued on shore, and lay at the Ship and Castle; but went every day to wait on my mistress. At last the ship was ordered into dock, where my master set me to work, which was to saw some wood up, and bring it home to his lodgings; however, I was ordered to lie on board, and come on shore every morning, which I was very glad of, because I thought in that case nobody would interrupt me.

One day wanting to put on a clean shirt before I came from aboard, I found my shirts were all wet; notwithstanding which, I did not stop to dry the one I used, but very unadvisedly put it on as it was, and went on shore. I had not been long there till I was seized with the rheumatism to such a degree that I was carried on board; and next day grew so very ill, that the doctor told me I must go to the hospital.

At this time my master had procured a boat to carry his things from the ship to his lodgings; whereupon the doctor's mate asked my master if he would let him have the boat, with two or three hands to carry me to the hospital? To which he consented, and sent one J___n B___n, the carpenter's mate, and the doctor's mate, whose name was Mr. L___e. I was then carried up to the agent in the hospital, and he ordered me to be taken into the fifth ward south, where I was put to bed very bad, and grew worse and worse every day; and at length became so delirious, that I neither knew what I said, or to whom I spoke. In this condition I remained till they thought it necessary to bleed me, by which I received great relief.

Being now grown a little better, I got up, but was not able to walk much; however, I recovered the use of my hands, and mended by degrees. When I was able to walk about the room, it came into my head, that I would try to go down stairs; and having got as far as the stair-case, the wind blew so cold, that I thought it would cut me asunder; therefore I was obliged to go back again into my ward. The nurse asked me how far I had been? I told her, as far as the stair-case; but felt it so very cold, that I could venture no farther. She then told me the danger I was in of catching cold again, which determined me not to attempt going again till the weather was finer.

While I continued here, the Sandwich sailed from Spithead to the Nore, with orders to go to Rochelle; but being sick, my master went and left me behind.

The weather now proving warmer, I endeavoured a second time to go down stairs. But when I came to the stair case, I found I was not able; for I could not bend my knees. I therefore sat down on the stairs, and slid from one step to the other till I got to the foot, which was very trouble-some for me before I could effect it. I then went under one of the arches where the sun shone warmest.

Being now pretty well recovered, they sent me on board the Royal Sovereign, a guard ship at Spithead, as a supernumerary man, which I was glad of; for soon after admiral Geary and all his servants came on board, whom I knew; and they were glad to see me. There was one John Grant who had a woman on board with him, and one George Robinson, a quarter-master, both of whom invited me to mess with them. I was very glad of the offer; because I then thought I should have some tea, as there would be a woman in the company. The quarter-master was likewise very kind to me; for he always keep some tea and sugar partly on my account; and we often drank tea together.

I shall now return to my former relation concerning my being admitted into the mess, which I continued in for some time. The young woman and I were very intimate, and she was exceeding fond of me; so that we used to play together like young children, insomuch that our messmates believed we were too familiar together; but neither of us regarded their surmises; and if they said any thing to her, she told them that if any thing like what they suspected had passed between us, the same should be practised in future. However, when John Grant became acquainted that she and I were so fond of each other's company, he began to be somewhat displeased; nevertheless, he was afraid to take any notice of it, lest his messmates should laugh at him; yet though he seemed to wink at it, he shewed her several tokens of this resentment, by beating her, and otherwise using her very ill, threatening to send her on shore.

Soon after this I received a letter from my parents, which gave me great pleasure, the contents of which are as follows:

"*Dear Child,*   *Ash, May 22, 1761.*

I received your letter very safe, and hope these few lines will find you in good health, as we are at present, thanks be to God for it. I would not have you believe that I thought it was too much trouble to write to you, since I am very glad to find you are in good health. But still, my dear child, when I think about you, it makes me almost distracted to reflect on your present situation, and the hardships you must needs go through. These thoughts, I say, make my heart ready to burst. However, I hope you will study to put your trust in God, who will help you in all your difficulties; and also flatter myself, that I shall have the pleasure of seeing you some time or other. All friends send their kind love to you, wish you well out of all your troubles, and desire you will write as soon as convenient. Your brother and sister send their kind love to you. I shall now conclude with our parental affection and blessing, from

"*Your afflicted Father and Mother,*
"*WM. and MARY LACY.*"

When I had read the above letter, I again condemned myself for the sorrow I had brought on my parents, by running away from them, which I was the sole cause of; for if I had made them acquainted with my design, they in all probability would have prevented it. May these bad effects of my rash conduct serve as a caution to forward children to mind their parents in their youthful days, which may prove to them a means of escaping many dangers they may be exposed to; and thus, by obedient behaviour, they will bring comfort on their aged parents heads, instead of grief and affliction as I did.

I proceed now to farther instances of my folly. While I was standing one day on the deck, the boatswain's mate desired me to go down to the yeoman for a bucket. As I was going to the store-room, the men were scraping the side of the ship; the ports being open on one side and shut on the other, and the men drawing water out of the hold, I perceived I could not go down there; however, the gratings being open, I thought I would jump over the cable, the consequence of which imprudence was, I fell down the forehold with my head upon the chime of a cask, and cut a terrible wound in it, which laid it quite open. When my messmates came down and beheld me, they were so frightened that they knew not what to do; however, they carried me into the cockpit to the doctor's mate, who bled and dressed my head, but was forced to sew it up with three stitches. During the time he did this, I was senseless; and when I came to myself, I was very apprehensive lest the doctor, in searching for bruises about my body, should discover that I was a woman; but it fortunately happened, he being a middle aged gentleman, was not very inquisitive; and my messmates being advanced in years, and not so active as young people, did not tumble me about to undress me.

As it was next to a miracle my sex was not discovered on the above occasion, I esteemed it a singular mercy God had prevented it at that time. The pain in my head, in consequence of the fall, was so exceedingly bad, that I was almost deprived of my senses; yet, notwithstanding my pain and illness, I had a continual fear upon me of being found out: and as I lay in my hammock, I was always listening to hear what they said, or whether they had made any discovery. My apprehensions were soon afterwards removed, on finding they were as ignorant as before, with respect to that particular; so that I continued in my hammock very easy and satisfied.

When one Mr. P___g___e, the doctor, came on board, he ordered my hammock to be lowered; and after dressing my head, he left me to the care of my messmates, who accordingly attended upon me.

There was at that time a bumboat woman on board, who gave me some tea and cake, and was otherwise very good to me. Her kindness was the more acceptable, as my teeth were grown so loose in my head, that I could not eat any thing; but by the care of this woman, I wanted for nothing; and in a short time found myself so much recovered, that I could go to the doctor, and have my head dressed every day. He often told me that he should give me the St. Andrew's Cross, which made me afraid to go afterwards, lest he should cut me. However, as he perceived I was in a fair way of being cured, I escaped the operation.

Once on the doctor's mate dressing my head, he bound it up so very tight, that it ached prodigiously; and I was not able to bear it. For this reason I went to him myself, desired he would look at my head, and told him it pained me so much that I fearcely knew how to sustain it. His answer was, he could not open it. Whereupon I went away as I came: but in a little time after, I found myself obliged to go to the doctor again, and tell him, that if he would not open it, I must endeavour to find somebody else that would. After hearing me express myself in this peremptory manner, he began to look at my head, and by loosening the bandage, gave me great ease, and removed the excruciating pain which the tightness had occasioned.

I then went to bed, and was taken so ill of a fever, that I became senseless for three or four days. The doctor perceiving this, told my messmates he would have me conveyed to the hospital in the morning, if I grew no better. They replied, he should not send me there, alledging, it would be the only way to put a final period to my existence, if I was carried into the cold. But it pleased God to remove the fever in a short time; so next day when the doctor came, and found it had left me, he thought I should soon recover my wonted health and strength. During the time of the fever, the doctor's mate let me blood, as I found afterwards, by my garter upon the orifice, which put me in great fear, lest he had discovered my sex. But when he came next to see me, he did not mention a word concerning that, which I am sure he would, had he known I had been a woman.

I now grew better every day; and if I had had a friend, I could have procured a smart ticket for Chatham, and should have received four pounds a year, or something more: But I was at that time utterly ignorant of such a provision; and had nobody to advise or direct me about it, my master being gone to sea. But by the blessing of God, I was at last better provided for.

As soon as I was pretty well recovered, I went to work again; and in a short time time was as well as ever. I was very sorry to find that my messmate George Robinson had left the ship, as I knew not what was become of him, nor have I heard of him since. This occasioned me to get a new messmate, which was the captain of the forecastle, whose name was Philip M__t__n, who had a notable woman to his wife. They were worth money, and lived very happy together on board the ship; and indeed few in our circumstances lived so comfortably as we did. This woman used to wash for me, and also for impressed men as they came on board; and if I did any work for these pressed men, my messmates would tell them they must pay me for it, because I had no friend in the world to help me: so that when I had done any thing for them, one would give me a pair of stockings, another breeches, and the rest would supply me in return with other necessaries; therefore I wanted for nothing of that sort.

The boatswain observing me so very tractable, by which I gained the good will of every body, seemed desirous I should come and mess with him, which appeared very strange to me, because he never knew me before: however, I soon found out the cause, which was as follows: There being a quarter-master's wife on board that came from the Isle of Wight, who sold all manner of things; and being a particular acquaintance of the boatswain's, she urged him to ask me to mess with him, in order to look after her things. But at that time I had an opportunity of doing something more serviceable for myself, than barely looking after their matters, which was, to go down into the school to learn to write and cast accompts.

Some time after this, having gone through a great deal of trouble, by serving different persons on board, my whole endeavour being always employed to please and assist every body as well as I could; at length, being induced by the boatswain's repeated acts of kindness to me, I came to a resolution of messing with him whenever he should hint the matter again, which he soon did: and indeed I afterwards found I had exchanged messmates to my own ease and advantage. He being very kind to me, I lived extremely happy; for as he did not come on board above once or twice a week, I had but little else to do than make his bed, and dress him a bit of victuals; so that I had time enough to wait upon the women. The boatswain's wife, who was a handsome woman, coming on board with her father and mother, I was ordered to dress some fish for them, which they were pleased to say were very well served up, and gave me sixpence as a gratuity for my trouble and care. He told me at the same time, that he would procure leave for me to go on shore from time to time; but I never had the good fortune to find that he performed this promise.

I had now been on board the Royal Sovereign one year and near seven months, when I received a letter from my master, which I here present to you, and is as follows:

"*From on board the Sandwich, Basque Road.*

"*William,*   *Oct. 2, 1762.*

I have taken this opportunity to write to you, to let you know that very shortly we expect to come to Spithead, and then hope to hear a good account of you; which if I do, will perform my promise, to put you to 'prentice in Chatham Yard, it you like it. Give my compliments to Mr. Jennings, the carpenter on board your ship; and you may shew him this letter if you please. I would have you be good; and take great care of yourself. The last time I heard from your mistress, she was very well. Take no cloaths from the captain; if you do, I shall not get your wages. So no more at present, from

    Your's, etc.
    "*RICH. BAKER.*"

This letter, according to my master's instructions, I shewed the carpenter and boatswain, who said my master promised very fair; and observed I had no reason to be afraid of having a bad name, for every body that knew my behaviour and conduct, would speak well of me. It gave me great pleasure to hear from my master; and when the Sandwich came, that the peace would be concluded.

Soon after this, the boatswain told me that all the ships were going into harbour to be paid off, and that the Sovereign would be the first; which induced me to think of engaging as an apprentice to my master at Chatham, though it did not entirely suit my inclination, because I knew there would be many persons at that place who were acquainted with me, and by that means I might soon be discovered: therefore I did not chuse to go to Chatham with him, but was rather willing to take my chance at Portsmouth.

It was not long before the Royal Sovereign was ordered into harbour to be paid off, but the St. George was the first ship, and ours the next. The boatswain told me to make myself easy, for I should stay with him till the Sandwich came in, and if she went to Plymouth, he would send me down in her. In a little time after, the ship was paid off; and it was not long before I went on shore, which I was very glad of; and my joy was so great on this occasion, that I ran up and down, scarcely knowing how to contain myself.

I had now been on board the Royal Sovereign one year, and almost nine months, without being on shore all the time; nor was I in the least suspected of being a woman. On December 21st, 1762, I went to the boatswain's house, and eat and drank there; this being much about Christmas time, the weather was very cold. As I was going down the town, I met the cockswain of the cutter to the Sandwich, which very much surprised me. I immediately asked him whether he belonged at that time to the Sandwich? Why yes, I do; and your master ordered me to tell you to come on board to see him. I told him, I could not come till to-morrow. After I parted from him, I went and informed the boatswain that the Sandwich was arrived, and that my master had sent for me to come on board; and also mentioned to him that I would go in the morning.

Being determined to write to my father and mother that day, it being nine months since they had heard from me: accordingly I sent them a letter, the purport of which is as follows:

Portsmouth Harbour,   *Dec. 25, 1762.*

    "*Hond. Father and Mother,*

This comes with my kind duty to you, and hope these few lines will find you in good health, as I am at present, thanks be to God for it. I am sorry to trouble you so much with writing; but your not answering my last letter, in acquainting me how you both are, makes me very uneasy. My master is just come home; and I shall go on board to him very soon. I am lately come on shore from the Royal Sovereign; and long very much to see you both; but must wait with patience. Pray give my love to my brother and sister, and all friends, together with my duty and prayers for your preservation.

"Your most undutiful Daughter,
"MARY LACY.

N.B. Please to direct to me as follows, For William Chandler, on board the Royal Sovereign, in Portsmouth Harbour.

These were the contents of the letter which I sent to my father and mother on this occasion; and, as I intimated before, that I should go on board to my master in the morning, accordingly I went down to the point, and seeing a barge I thought was the captain's, but it proved to be his clerk's, I asked the favour to let me go on board with him, which he readily complied with. This was immediately after Christmas-day. Having got safe on board, I went directly to my master's cabbin, where I found both him and the gunner, who were very glad to see me. As soon as my old friend Jeremiah Paine came, who was formerly my fellow-servant, my master gave him a bottle of wine to make ourselves both merry, in telling our adventures concerning what had passed and happened to each other since our last parting.

Soon afterwards my master sent for me, and asked me whether we had drank out the wine, and eat the plum-pudding he ordered? I told him, we had. He then renewed his old story of telling the gunner that he would put me apprentice in the yard, with such other specious promises as he had often made me before. I thanked him heartily for his good will, and endeavours to serve me. Having ended this story, he began with another, which was an account of the loss he had met with since he had been at sea: but this will more properly appear in another place.

After this I went on shore to Mr. Dawkins the boat-swain, and told him what my master had said to me, which he approved of, and observed, that he hoped my master would not take me up to Chatham, and there leave me, without binding me 'prentice; for, says he, if he does, he will be very unjust to you.

I next went on board the Royal Sovereign to see after my box, and other things, which I brought on shore, and afterwards went to my master, who told me that my mistress was come thither in order to go to Plymouth; for his son was arrived there as carpenter of the Bienfaisant, and lay in sick quarters, and at the point of death; but before she could get an opportunity of seeing him he died, which was a melancholy circumstance to his father and mother, he being their only son.

When my mistress had taken an account of her deceased son's effects, she returned to Portsmouth. But the afflicted parents were so overwhelmed with grief and sorrow for the loss of their child, that their case excited compassion in every one present. Having settled their affairs here, my master and mistress went to lodge at the sign of the Ship and Castle. But I was kept constantly employed in going backwards and forwards, sometimes on board, and at others on shore to light his fire, besides doing the other common business of a lodging.

My master still continued talking to me about placing me out as an apprentice as soon as we got to Chatham; whereupon my mistress remarked, that such an action as that, could it be accomplished, would be greatly for my advantage; though by the way, she seemed very far from approving of it in general. Perceiving her inclination with respect to the matter, I thought it was a very fit opportunity for me to get clear of the apprenticeship. So when my master asked me if I would go to Chatham with him, I bluntly told him I would not; for I thought myself too old to go 'prentice. Well, said he, William, I will send your money down to one Mr. John Lucas, when I get up to Chatham. However, this promise he never performed; for he only wrote to Mr. Lucas concerning the money due to me whilst on board the Royal Sovereign, which he had no manner of business with. But the captain kept me upon the books, and paid me; which the former never did to this day.

My master and mistress being gone to Chatham, I went on board the Royal Sovereign again, was entered there as purser's servant, and had liberty to leave the ship when I pleased. I continued here a month, employed by men and officers, in going on shore for their necessaries: so that by frequently rowing in the boat, I became perfectly acquainted with the nature and management of it.

One day as I was going on shore with the boatswain of the Sandwich, he very seriously asked me if I would go 'prentice to the carpenter off the Royal William, whose name was Mr. M'Clean? I told him, I would let him know tomorrow; for I did not know how to deny him, being afraid they would mistrust me if I evaded it. Accordingly I went to Mr. Dawkins, the boatswain of the Royal Sovereign, and told him what Mr. Summers, the boatswain of the Sandwich, had said to me: whereupon he advised me to agree to the proposal; for that it was better to have some trade, than none at all; and added, I know him to be a good tempered man; and seven years is not for ever, so I would have you go. But the dread of being discovered that I was a woman before the expiration of my apprenticeship, was a great obstacle to this proposal.

The next day according to my promise I went on shore, and saw Mr. M'Clean waiting for Mr. Seamer to introduce me to him; for we were unacquainted with each other. In a short time after he came to me, and asked if I would go 'prentice? I told him I would. While we were thus talking, Mr. M'Clean came up to me, and asked if I would be his apprentice? I answered, Yes, Sir. Well, young man, said he, will you go on board with me? I told him I would, provided he would let me have a boat to go on board the Royal Sovereign. Young man, he returned, you shall have a boat, and the boys shall go thither to assist you. Accordingly I went and brought my chest, bed, and bedding, on board the Royal William.

My master had another boy out at sea, who was not big enough to work as an apprentice in the yard, nor would the builder agree to take him; however, his own parents being dead, and his father-in-law taking no proper care of him, my master very generously maintained him.

I thought till about this time that my master was a married man; for he had a woman on board with him, and a girl that was her daughter. But I soon had reason to believe they were not married, from her impudent behaviour, having had frequent opportunities of making particular observations on the conduct of loose women, and could discern their vicious inclinations immediately.

I had now been on board some time before I was bound apprentice: but the woman who co-habited with my master, began in a little time to be so familiar with me, that I thought it very extraordinary a woman who was an entire stranger to me, should become so suddenly enamoured.

Soon after this my master ordered me to clean myself, and be ready to go ashore with him, as he designed to bind me 'prentice that very day, which was the 4th of March, 1763. A boat (though it was not the proper harbour boat) being now alongside the ship to receive us, according to my master's directions, I immediately made myself ready, and prepared to go; but as this boat of ours was very old, and not capable of carrying much sail, especially when it blew a little fresh; and there being moreover a pretty brisk gale of wind, we had a great deal of trouble to reach the shore. My master then stood for the Sandwich, and went on board, as the boat was going on shore. We left our boat at the stern of the Sandwich, and went in theirs: but the wind blew so hard that we could not reach the hulk, but were forced to go to the north jett, where some caulkers stages lay alongside, at which place they had driven some nails into the piles (to climb up by) instead of ropes, which were at least sixteen feet high.

My master and the gunner had got safely up, and were walking on; but when I had almost climbed to the top, letting go the rope to take hold of the ring-bolt, my foot slipped, and I fell down into the sea; but as soon as I appeared again, the boys upon the stage soon pulled me up, though I was wet from head to foot; however, I recovered myself as well as I could.

Presently after this sad disaster my master and the gunner began to miss me; and coming back to see where I was (observing me on the stage) asked the reason why I had been so long in coming? I then told them that I had fell overboard. On which my master laughed, and sent me to a blacksmith's shop, where I immediately pulled off my coat and waistcoat to dry myself; after which he brought me out of the yard, and gave me something hot to drink, to wet the inside, for the outside was sufficiently soaked before.

My master and I went together to wait on the builder, to know if he approved of me for an apprentice; but he not being in the office, we went to his house. On asking if he was at home, the servant told us he was, and called him to us. My master then asked him, how he liked me for an apprentice? Why, said the builder, I like him very well; for I think he is a stout lad. So my master had me entered; but not as a yard servant, as he was not allowed two, being only carpenter of the Deptford, a fourth-rate man of war. At this time he did duty on board the Royal William, the carpenter of which was dead, and he had some hopes of procuring the place for himself.

I shall now proceed to relate in what manner I went to work in the yard. My master began to enquire for a quarterman for me to work under; accordingly he went to one Mr. Dunn, and found him in his cabbin. After paying his compliments, he told him he had brought him a new hand, and that he hoped I should be a good boy. (And indeed I must confess he gave me a good character): and at the same time told Mr. Dunn that he hoped he would put me under a skilful workman to learn my trade; which Mr. Dunn engaged his word and honour to do: For you must know that I was a cadet, to work one week in the yard, and another on board a new ship, the Britannia, just launched. There being an overflowing in the harbour, all the carpenters and servants were ordered to open the men of war, to let air in, and keep the ships from rotting: But this did not last long, for we only went in the morning and evening; so that we were in the yard the greatest part of the day.

Mr. Dunn put me under one Mr. Cote to learn my business, who was a very good-tempered man, and took great pains to instruct me; he liked me very well, and seemed to be greatly delighted to hear me talk.

This affair being thus far concluded, my master went and bought me a saw, an ax and chizzel, which made me very proud to think I had got some new tools to work with. On shewing them to the man I served under, he told me he would put some new shafts to them; which pleased me very well, thinking that would be very serviceable to me in beginning to learn my trade.

The first work I began upon was, to bore holes in the bottom of the ship called the Thunderer, which, as I was at first unacquainted with the method of doing it, proved hard work for me. This occasioned me to think I should not be able to serve out my time without being discovered.

My master and mistress living at this time on board the Royal William, I had no house on shore to reside in, and was therefore obliged to go on board every night; so that the boys on board our ship had a great deal of trouble to fetch me backwards and forwards: however, I soon began to lessen their trouble, by taking an opportunity to go back again in the shipwright's boat. But when it was my week to be on board, my master frequently sent me to fetch beer and other necessaries, sometimes with and sometimes without money, just as it suited his humour. However, as it happened, the ship did not lie a great way from shore, and the place where we landed was called the Hardway.

I must here observe, that the boatswain had a canoe, which I was very fond of making use of, though if I stept ever so little on one side she would overset. I continued for some time to pass and repass in her; and having learned by frequent practice the right method of rowing, could make her run with surprising expedition.

One day my master came to the yard in four-oar'd boat, and said he wanted me on board, bidding me get my ship ready. Accordingly I got into my canoe, and my master into his four-oar'd boat, when he told me he would row with me for sixpence. I replied, I would; but if I got on board first, I would insist on having the money. He promised I should. I then went alongside their boat with my canoe, that is to say over-against them; after which we started, and plied our oars as fast as we could. To enable me to proceed with greater ease and expedition, I pulled off my waistcoat, quickly overtook them, and got first on board; which when I had done, I fell a laughing at them, and called out, Where's my money, where's my money! He told me I should have it. But, instead of giving it me, in the evening he took all on shore and spent it among us. From this time my master every now-and-then challenged me to row with him; which I told him I was very willing to do whenever he was disposed for it, provided he would pay me the money when he lost. My mistress observed at the same time, that he did not do well in refusing to pay me, as he had engaged to do it.

At this time there were on board our ship a deputy purser's wife, with one Mr. Robinson and his wife, all acquaintances of my mistress, who were brought up together at Gosport. As I was then on board, they sent me for some liquor, and would often get as drunk together as David's sow: and in the height of these frolicks, they would often say, "Ay, he is, ay he is, the best boy on board." In regard to mother Robinson, I must acknowledge, she would do any kind office for me. Indeed I was in general well beloved by the women, if by nobody else; and, thank God, greatly respected by my master: so that I lived a quite happy life; and went to work at the yard every day.

When we went to work on board the Niger frigate, I had a tool-chest made; and the quarterman, a person that I worked with, was very kind to me. I had my provisions of the king; so we made one allowance serve us, and sold the other to the purser for a guinea a quarter, as we both often dined at my master's house.

When I worked in the dock-yard, I used to sell my chips at the gate; and sometimes would carry a bundle to Mr. Dawson, the boatswain, and was always welcome to his house whenever I pleased: Besides, my master frequently asked me to dine with him on Sunday, if they had any company on board, and then I got a sufficiency; for he would always have me wait at table. While I was laying the cloth, my mistress would stroke me down the face, and say, I was a clever fellow. Which expression made me blush.

Frequently after supper my master would ask me to favour them with a song, adding, that if I condescended to this, it would oblige them very much. Wherefore to divert them, I commonly sung them two or three songs, which often made them merry, till about twelve o'clock; when my master would order me with three more boys to row them to the Hard at Portsmouth Common; after which they made us a present to buy a little beer; but we made all the haste back we could.

I continued working in the dock; and my master and mistress were very fond of my company, because I could sing to please them. When I came home in the evening, I generally sat down by them, and sung a merry song, with which they were greatly delighted; so that I thought it no manner of trouble to serve them either by day or night.

And thus having the good will of all, I lived very happy.

One evening my master had some company came on board to see him, and I was appointed to wait at table. When my mistress kept calling so repeatedly, I concluded my master was not married to her: This suspicion occasioned me to observe to my fellow-servant, (whose name was Jonathan Lyons) that I thought they were not man and wife; at which he fell a laughing: however, I did not care speak much about it, lest I should not say right. So it passed on for some time.

A little while afterwards, coming on board in the evening, my master and mistress had some words; and the woman that was acquainted with my mistress, let me into the secret of their intimacy. You must know, said she, your mistress, as you call her, was never married to your master, nor ever will, for she is at present married to another; her lawful husband lives at this time at Greenwich Hospital, and his name is Mr. ___.

To proceed with the rest of my adventures. My master having no other ship, we lived on board; though he often talked of taking a house on shore, which (by the way) my fellow servants and myself heartily wished he would do. But he now began to take more and more notice of me every day; yet he was very kind to us; and would not allow me to clean his shoes, nor the knives and forks, or do any thing when I came home from the dock-yard, except when there were company on board, and then I waited at table.

It appeared my master formed a strong suspicion that I had got a sweetheart who lived upon the Common, and was often talking about it, advising me to be cautious, and not to marry till I was out of my time; and then he would give me a wedding dinner. Indeed I often laughed to myself, when I considered that my master imagined I went a courting; for I was acquainted with several young women, which occasioned him to think that I was rather too familiar with them: and truly very glad I was he thought so; for in that case he could have no mistrust of my sex.

One day when I was on board, and my master shore, my mistress and Mr. Robinson were disposed to make themselves merry: accordingly they sent me to shore to fetch some liquor, which they repeated so often that I was quite tired; and kept it up till they had spent all their money, but did not know where to get more: and I remember, that I once mentioned in their hearing, my going to one Mr. Penny to bring liquor for my master on credit. This opportunity they thought was a specious pretext to get more liquor. My mistress therefore sent me for a pint of rum, and desired me to tell them, my master would pay for it when he came on shore. Accordingly I went and brought the rum; imagining, that as my master allowed me to call her mistress, he would not blame me for fetching it, having given me no orders to the contrary. So that, according to the proverb, with this liquor they got as drunk as pipers.

On my master's coming on board in the evening, he soon perceived what they had been at; but took no notice, only sat and laughed at them, he being very well acquainted with their frolicks. But they were so pleased with me for bringing this liquor, that my fellow servants seemed almost to envy me; and said, they believed my mistress and I were too intimate, and that they wished she was so fond of them; for they observed, she was always giving me something or other, and that it was enough to spoil the most sober man in the world, because she would never go on shore but I must go with her, and then went in all sorts of company, both good and bad. But, thank God, it happened very well for me, as I never went to these licentious places but it occasioned me to be very much on my guard, and to be extremely cautious what sort of company I kept.

I must here reflect with gratitude, that if some sort of people had been witness to the variety of scenes of life that have passed under my observation, the fight would have made their very hair stand on end: Some were quarrelling and fighting; others had their eyes knocked out, and afterwards kicked out of doors; and sometimes even driven from their warm beds, and had no person of reputation or humanity to receive them. Therefore all these disagreeable prospects should teach us to amend in ourselves what we see amiss in others. These considerations occasioned me often to think with great sorrow, that I had done mischief enough in leaving my parents, without their knowledge or consent; and hope this will be an example to all others not to be guilty of the like imprudence.

I shall now proceed (according to my journal) to relate what passed concerning the pint of rum I brought to my mistress; for my master had been on shore to pay the beer, but not the rum: Mr. Penny, it appears, had then given him to understand, that there was a pint of rum to pay. A pint of rum, said my master! I have had none. Do you know who came for it? Yes, replied Mr. Penny, I know the boy when I see him. Upon that my master came on board, and asked if we had fetched any rum on board for any body from Mr. Penny's? They all answered, No. He then said, I shall find it out; therefore you had better let me know before I go on shore. Hearing this, I went and told my mistress what had passed on the occasion; but she would not suffer me to tell him till we went on shore.

My master soon after ordered us all to go on shore along with him: He going first into the house where we had the beer and rum, found there the carpenter of the Thunderer, who was present when I fetched the rum; but he would say nothing to my master, lest he should affront my mistress, because she was a very good customer. Upon this we were called in, when my master asked Mr. Penny which of us all it was that brought the rum? Mr. Penny began at top, and narrowly examining the physiognomy and habit of every one till he came to me, then said, This is the boy who fetched it. My master then said, William, did you fetch it? Yes, Sir, returned I; but I shall be glad to speak with you. Hereupon we both went out. Well, said he, did your mistress send you for any rum? I told him, Yes. Why, says he, did you not tell me before you came on shore? Because, I replied, my mistress would not let me; though I was sure you would soon find it out. Well, says my master, go in and get some beer. Accordingly we went in, and got two or three pots of beer, and then went on board again.

After this my mistress came to me, and asked if my master had found it out? Found it out! Said I, yes, to be sure he has; and you had better have let me told him before I went on shore, and then no one would have known any thing of the matter; but now every body knows it. Soon after my master came on board, but took no notice of the above-mentioned affair.

He began now to think of taking a house on the Hardway, for he heard there was one to lett, which we were glad of. I still went to the yard to work; but was forced to go round to Gosport, which was two full miles walk twice every day. And after I got home in the evening, was forced to hail the ship; and when the wind was in the east they could not hear me; therefore I was often obliged to stand in the wind and cold till I was almost froze to death; which made me think how happy I should be if my master had but a house; for then I should have a good fire to sit by, and victuals to eat till the boat came for me.

I used every now-and-then to go on board with my canoe; and there were three apprentices that were very idle, who would take my canoe to go perrywinkling; having therefore all got into her, with a bucket to hold the perrywinkles, they set off, and got a great many, with which they returned, and came alongside the ship; but beginning to play their pranks, they overset her, lost all the perrywinkles, and narrowly escaped being drowned, though two of them could swim, who getting at last alongside the ship, with our assistance got on board. It was with much difficulty we saved poor Abraham Mills, who was very near drowned; and my canoe left bottom upwards. These boys were continually plaguing me to go with them; but I was always afraid, lest they should overset her, for the least thing would do it: so that I never had the courage to venture with them; and whenever they got in first to go on shore, I would go in the harbour boat; and on our return, would get in my canoe and go on board.

It came now to my turn to keep watch at night, when my master ordered me to watch four hours, and then call somebody else. Mine being the middle watch, I was ordered to strike the bell every half an hour. Accordingly I went forwards, and struck as I was directed. However, being but a cadet in the yard, my master ordered me to go a fishing with him in Stock bay, when he caused me to sit down all the way backwards and forwards to sing. One day it being very wet, the fish began to bite very fast, and my master would not leave off till the tide obliged him to retire. We the weighed, set our sails, got safe into the harbour, and safe on board, though in a very wet condition.

Sunday following, my master had given an invitation to an old landlord and his family (where he once lodged) to come and take a dinner with him on board; therefore he ordered me and my fellow servant to go and fetch them from the shore. I immediately cleaned myself, put on my blue jacket, went for them, and rowed them to the ship; and while they were at dinner, I waited at table. My mistress asked them how they liked me? Why I think, said they, that he is a very handy lad. To which my mistress answered, Ay, and he is a sweet tempered lad too: for she was then in good humour; and made me eat and drink of all that was prepared for the guests.

When the evening was come, we prepared to row the visitors on shore again; and as the wind began to blow pretty fresh, I haled the boat alongside the ship, put the mast and sails up, and set sail. We had a fair wind to the shore, and landed them at the place where we took them from in the morning: we afterwards tried to work out from the shore, and tack about backwards and forwards, but could make no way, which obliged us to lower the sails, and pull the boat out to the stern of the Essex, and then hoist sail again; but the wind being north-west, was right against us, and blew so hard that we could not carry sail enough to work on the other shore. However, we ventured to sail; but when we got over against the hulk, there came a squall of wind, which almost overset us. I had got the main sheet in one hand, and the tiller in the other; but I let them go, and luffed her up, as she was almost full of water, being very old, and not having ballast enough to carry much sail. In this distress I struck sail, and let her drive where she would. We then drove down Palchester lake, where fortunately for us a lighter lay moored, on board of which was a man, who seeing us coming, hove out a rope, which I caught hold of, took a turn with it, and moored her to the lighter. We then went on board, and staid all night; for we were as wet as we possibly could be, not having so much as a dry thread about us. As there was no fire, we were forced to sit up all night in our cloaths; and thanks be to God we were so well off, seeing it was a great mercy we were not drowned.

My master rose in the morning, and looked about the harbour to try if he could see or hear any thing of us. Getting no intelligence of us, he began to be frightened, and at length concluded we were drowned. But I had ample reason to be thankful to Divine Providence, which had preserved me in all my extremity and trouble, and continued to help me; for we bailed the water out of the boat, and then rowed up to the ship. Before we came on board, we saw our master looking out of the stern gallery; who perceiving us coming, made up a large fire for us as soon as we came on board, and gave me a pair of dry stockings to put on.

Having got some dry cloaths, my master and I went to the dock-yard, but too late for my call: whereupon I went to the clerk, who taking my checque off, I went to work till night. When I came on board in the evening, I was very glad to sit down by the fire; but did not sit there long before I turned into my hammock; for being greatly fatigued, I found I wanted rest most, and could sleep without rocking, having been up all night before.

It unfortunately happened that I could not continue to work in the yard, as I wanted to do, being obliged to go to work with my master every other week on board the ships, which in a great measure hindered me from learning my trade. I therefore asked my master to let me go into the yard to work. He told me the yard was so far off, that it was not worth my while to go down to work. I observed to him, that as I met with so many interruptions, I should never be able to learn my trade. Well, said he, if you don't learn to build, you will learn to pull pieces: for it seems my master expected to be the carpenter of the Royal William, having done duty on board her for some time: in that case he was to have two boys allowed him in the yard; this, however, never happened; one Mr. Williams being appointed for her. I afterwards learned he was to have a third rate, which has as many boys as a second-rate, tho' there is ten shillings difference.

My master had now obtained a warrant for a new ship that was building at Lippe, called the Europa; and, coming home one night, I happened to be on shore, when he said to me, Well, master Chandler, what news now! Sir, I replied, I don't hear of any. Why, said he, have not you heard that you and I are to go to plough, and that I am to hold the plough, and you drive the horses? I found he was only joking; because he had got a new ship building in the country at Lippe.

Next time I had occasion to go to the dock, wanting to come on board sooner than usual, I went in my canoe, and got alongside the shore; but the wind blowing pretty fresh, I could not keep her off the shore, nor get a head. Mr. Dawkins of the Royal Sovereign seeing me in distress, sent his four-oar'd boat to fetch me on board, otherwise I should certainly have been drowned. As I came by the ship, he said to me, Your canoe will be your coffin one day or other; and kindly added, if your boys are so lazy, that they will not carry you down to the dock in their duty-weeks, I will send my boy to fetch you. I returned him thanks for his kindness.

I shall next proceed to relate what passed concerning the young woman who lived at Mr. Dawkins's house, which place I often went to. Being there one evening, he asked me to stay till morning, as he himself was to remain on board all night; and moreover, the maid insisted on my promising to stay there. Having consented, we sat at cards till twelve o'clock; when some young women, who spent the evening with us, went home. I then asked the maid where I was to lie? She answered, There was no place but with her, or her mistress. I told her I would lie in her bed. Accordingly she lighted me up to her chamber. Perceiving her forwardness, I thought it was no wonder the young men took such liberties with the other sex, when they gave them such encouragement; and I am compelled, for the sake of truth, to say this much of the women; but am far from condemning all for the faults of one or two: however, when a young woman allows too much freedom, it induces the men to think they are all alike.

I must confess, that if I had been a young man, I could not have withstood the temptations which this young person laid in my way: for she was so fond of me, that I was ever at her tongue's end; which was the reason her master and mistress watched her so narrowly. In short, there was nothing I could ask that she would refuse; and, to make me the sensible of it, my shorts were washed and prepared for me in the very best manner she was able.

One day my master took me to task about keeping this young woman company; adding, that he was afraid she would be a means of corrupting my morals, since her brothers were given to dancing, and night-revelling. But when she asked me to go amongst them, I gave a flat denial on that head. She then enquired the reason why I would not go? I answered, That it generally brought young people into bad habits and company of loose behaviour, destroyed their constitution, and rendered them incapable (by being up all night) to do their business the following day. Finding me determined not to comply with her solicitation, she never after that time asked me to go with them.

I was now a yard servant; and lived at my master's house on shore, who told me that I should have a new suit of cloaths, and not go so shabby as I was. To this end he went to Mr. D___ge, a taylor in Gosport, and ordered him to come on Sunday morning to take measure of me for a new suit of cloaths. The taylor came as he was directed; and my master gave me my choice of the colour, for which I thanked him, and fixed upon a blue, which he seemed well pleased with: and I was not a little proud to think that I should have good and decent apparel to appear in, as I could then walk out on Sundays with the young women.

When I had got my new cloaths, one Edward Turner, who messed with me when I was on board, and between whom and myself there had always subsisted a very intimate friendship, came on shore, and invited me to walk out with him. Having first asked leave of my master, which he readily granted, we accordingly set out; and when in each others company, we were always talking about the young women, or of working in the yard; for Wednesday and Saturday being the womens chip days, I soon made myself acquainted with some of them; and found them at all opportunities as well pleased in procuring the acquaintance of the men as in any place in England.

One day the above-mentioned Edward Turner invited two young women to come and take a dinner with him and his messmate on board the Royal William; for on my coming to live on shore, he got another messmate to dine with him. On this occasion, my trusty friend Edward, asked me if I would come and dine with him at the same time and place? And then, says he, I will help you to a sweetheart. I told him, if my master would permit me to come, I certainly would. He accordingly gave me leave; and I immediately went down to Gosport on board the Royal William, that was brought into dock to have a thorough repair. But the young women not being come, I was very impatient till they arrived, for I wanted much to see them.

We had a leg of mutton and turnips, and a fine plum-pudding provided, with plenty of gin and strong beer, which I considered as a grand entertainment for me and the young ladies. I had not been long on board before they came; on the sight of whom, I went immediately and paid my compliments to them; and we soon became acquainted together, they not forgetting to ask where I lived, which I as readily told them. We were very merry with our new acquaintance; and I soon found that Vobbleton-street was the place of their residence. This street in Portsmouth-town is inhabited with divers classes of people; so that I soon found what sort of company I was with.

Having spent the day on board with a good deal of mirth and humour, we agreed to escort the young women home: and indeed it was very proper we should.

Having therefore trudged to town with them, we were prevailed upon by their importunities, to stay supper with them: so that with one thing or other, we tarried there so late, that we could not get a boat to carry us over the water; at which I began to fret, lest my master should severely reprimand me. For as I had my new cloaths on, and knew that I must go to the yard to work in the morning, it really made me very uneasy. However, to remove this difficulty, the young women insisted on our lying together at their house.

I knew not what to do in this case: but recollecting that this young man had no suspicion of my being a woman, we went to bed together; and lay till four o'clock in the morning, when we got up and went to dock. As we were walking along, he asked me what I thought of those girls, and how I liked them? I told him, I thought they were a couple of merry girls.

As soon as I came up to the place of call, the people began to stare at me, which brought scarlet in my face; and asked me where I had been all night? I made them no answer; only went to the clerk, to desire leave to go home and pull off my cloaths, and put others on to work with; which he readily granted.

After this, lest I should meet my master, I crossed the water: but I was no sooner got home than I found that he was gone round to look for me, thinking he would meet me coming round that way. I went up stairs, pulled off my cloaths, and put others on; and desired my master's nephew to take no notice to his uncle that I was come home; which he promised not to do. But my mistress neither hearing or seeing any thing of me, and being more inquisitive than usual, as soon as she got up in the morning, went up stairs, and looked in my chest; on seeing my cloaths there, she came down, and severely reproved the boy for not telling her of it.

In the evening when work was over, my fellow servant and I went home; and the first word my master said to me was, How do you do, master Chandler? I hope you and she lay very close together last night? No, Sir, I did not lie with any woman last night; for I lay with Edward Turner. I have only your bare word for that, said he. Sir, I replied, you may believe me if you please. My master, it is true, believed I was very fond of some young woman or other; and so I was; but not in that manner he thought I was guilty of. However, he was not angry with me for lying out all night; and I took pretty good care not to stay out again. As for my fellow servant, he was always asleep as soon as he came home from dock; and though we lay together six months, I was in no danger of his finding me out, as he was no sooner abed but asleep.

It now happened that my master's young nephew lay along with us; and I was more afraid of him than of the other, because he was not so sleepy; though I considered, that being so young, there could be no apprehension of danger from him.

My master asked me sometimes on a Sunday, whether I would go along with him, or meet my sweetheart? I often chose rather to accompany my master to Blocks fort, where we often staid some time; and I might eat or drink any thing I pleased; for he was a very good-natured man to me: notwithstanding which, there was one thing in him that I disliked, which was, that he would swear very much. This unjustifiable practice I was very averse to; and could not help thinking he was quite blameable in living with a woman as a wife, that was every day contributing to ruin him; for I often heard it reported, that he might have married with a woman of fortune, who in all likelihood would have made him a very happy man.

The pernicious effects of his criminal cohabitation with this person appeared in several instances, and particularly in the following one: In a short time after we came to live on shore, she used to fetch so much liquor in his name that he could scarcely discharge the debts she had contracted, which very frequently soured his temper, and occasioned him with some heat to tell her he would turn her out of doors; which made me think I should soon have a new mistress.

Some time after this, my master had some business at Blocks fort, and she determined to follow him, but with no other intention than to scandalize him in the worst manner she could, which produced a great many reproachful words betwixt them.

When my fellow-servant and I came home from work at night, we found the doors fast, which occasioned us to go to the next house to enquire if the key was there. The people told us my mistress had left it. Having got the key, we both went in, supped, and retired to bed; but had not been there long before our mistress came, and brought a waterman along with her; for she had been at Gosport amongst her old acquaintances. She soon called for me. I told her I was coming down; which I did without the knowledge of my bedfellow, who never heard me either get out of bed or in again; so that I could never have had a more agreeable bedfellow in my life: for if I has lain a-bed a week, and ever so earnestly wished for such a one, I could scarce have such another.

When I came down, I found the waterman along with my mistress, who began haleing and pulling me about in such a manner, that I could not tell what was the matter with her, or the reason for her doing so. Afterwards I found that she wanted some beer; for she said she was thirsty. Accordingly I went and brought a pot of ringwood: and it being summer time, she sat at the door to drink it; over against which there being a wheelbarrow, I went and sat down upon it. My mistress observing me, came and placed herself in my lap, stroking me down the face, telling the waterman what she would do for me: so that the few people present could not forbear laughing to see her sit in such a young boy's lap as she thought I was. However, she had not been long in this situation before my master came home, and passed by her as she sat there; but taking no notice that he saw us, went in doors. And indeed I was very much frightened lest he should beat me; but I thought he could not justify be angry with me, as it was all her own fault.

I went then to try the door, to discover if my master had locked it, which he had done; therefore I told her the door was locked, and that we must both lie in the street. Upon which, she said, She would go to Gosport, and that I should go along with her.

As we were thus talking together under the window, my master overhearing her say, She would set off for Gosport, was resolved to give us something, if it was only a good wetting, to remember him before we went; and accordingly in a moment he threw up the window, and soused us all over with a chamber-pot full of water; which made me fall into such a fit of laughter, that my sides were ready to burst. In short, I could not refrain from laughing, to see what a pickle she was in.

After this a thought came into my head that I would again try whether the door was locked before we set off for Gosport, and, as I wished, found it open. I did not stop to tell her of it, but immediately took off my shoes and stockings, ran up stairs, pulled my bedfellow out of his place, and got into it myself; for I supposed if my master came up to thresh me, he would lay hold of him first, and then I should have time to get away. However, as good luck would have it, he did not concern himself with me; but vented his anger on my mistress when she came in, telling her she might go to the waterman again, and would not let her come to bed.

In the morning my bedfellow John Lyons wondered how he came into my place; for he had heard nothing about the matter, being such a sound sleeper. We both went as usual to work at the dock. But when we came home I was under most terrible apprehensions that my master would chastize me; but to my great comfort, he did not seem to take the least notice of what had passed on the occasion. Having now given you some account of the behaviour and disposition of my mistress, I shall leave her for a while, and proceed to other occurrences.

My master found out at length that I had a sweetheart, who lived at Portsmouth Common, but in what part he could not tell, though he imagined he should find it out some time or other; but after all, he was mistaken in the person; for he thought of a young woman that lived in Hanover Row, which was the very house I went to; and therefore resolved one day or other to go at dinner time to enquire for me, imagining that to be the best time to find me there. Accordingly my master took an opportunity to go to the place where he believed I frequently resorted to; but when he went there, the people happened to be out.

When I came home at night from the dock, the first word he said to me was, Your servant, Mr. Chandler, pray how does your wife do, that is to be? For I have been at the house to-day, but the people were not at home; however, I suppose you know where they are gone to. At first I could not tell what he meant by it, not knowing that he had been at the house, or who had told him that I went there. I made answer, A wife, Sir! that is more than I think of yet. He then said, You can't make me believe so. Sir, said I, I don't know who you are talking about. No! replied he, don't you know the house that has steps to go up at the door? Steps to the door! said I, I don't know what you mean. Immediately upon that I recollected the house in Hanover Yard upon the Common; and asked him (describing such a house) if it was that he meant? O! said he, with a little raillery, you have thought of it at last. Which in fact was so far true: but I did not care who knew that I went there; for the woman was most certainly a very good friend to me, though she knew not what I was.

At last, my master said to me, Well, William I would have you stay till you are out of your time before you marry; and if she be a sober girl, I'll give you a wedding dinner. Indeed I could not help laughing at what he had said to me about going a courting; and I was very glad to find he thought so.

I now began frequently to talk to the young women, and soon became a tolerable proficient in the art of court-ship, but was very cautious of what I said to them; for our sex are so weak as to think that if a young man does but once speak to them, he must become a sweetheart at once. In this respect we are greatly deceived; but they who know as much of both sexes as I do, would be of a different opinion; therefore would not have you trust too far, lest you should be disappointed. But true it is, my master would ever be pestering me with something or other about the young women; and my mistress was so evil inclined, that she thought every body as bad as herself.

One night when I came home from work from the dock, I found myself pretty much indisposed, and seeming somewhat uneasy, I sat down to rest myself, which my mistress took the opportunity of making a ground of invective; for thinking I was fast asleep, she began to question my fellow-servant about the cause of my indisposition. He said, he knew nothing farther than that he herd me say, I was not well. Ay, said she, I am sure he is ill indeed, for he has no life in him; he never used to sit down sleeping in this manner before; little thinking I heard every word she uttered. When I began to move, she thus addressed me: Well, Bill, what is the matter? I told her, Nothing more ailed me than being a little sick, and out of order. She said, I am sorry for it; and declined making any more mention of her suspicions at this time: and for my part I took no farther notice of what passed. She, nevertheless, told my master a strange pack of stuff; but he had too much good sense to take notice of it.

When we sat down to supper, he would often say to me, Well, master Chandler, how do you find yourself now? I hope you are something better. Nor would my mistress be behindhand in her questions and insinuations; and frequently gave me very great liberty to be free with her, even more than I could wish to subscribe to, or acknowledge; but I took it from whence it came.

Thus much is certain, that she did not know what to think of me; but verily believed I kept company with the above-mentioned young woman in Hanover Row on the Common, though she was greatly deceived; for I seldom went out with any young woman except Elizabeth Cook, who being very fond of my company, would not leave me, which gave me some cause to believe the intimacy would bring trouble on me one day or other. I thought therefore, the best way to put an end to this matter, would be, to frame some cause of dislike in her conduct: to effect which, a very favourable opportunity soon offered; for going on board the Royal Sovereign to see her, where her master and mistress then were, I observed a man to be very familiar with her: and in truth, her master himself, who was frequently giving me the most wholesome instructions, seemed very glad of the occasion to mention to me a hint of their too great familiarity.

One evening I went to the house of the young woman's father, and asked for Miss Betsy. Her mother answered, She was gone out; but she expected her home very soon. I therefore waited till her return, when we took a walk together.

After a little conversation, by way of prelude to my design, I told her, I thought it would be best for us to break off acquaintance; because it plainly appeared to me, I was not the only person she gave her company to, mentioning at the same time what I saw on board the Royal Sovereign.

On this, she seemed greatly confused; and asked what I could mean by questioning her constancy; adding, that she never once entertained so much as a single thought about any person besides myself, and that if I would promise her marriage she would not grudge to stay twelve years for me. To which I made no other reply than that from what I had already seen, I ran the risque of buying a bad bargain, and then I should be in an unhappy situation indeed. Notwithstanding all this, she was determined not to quarrel with me on any pretence: so that not knowing what to do with her, it passed off for that time; and we still continued our walks as opportunity served.

Soon after this, some misunderstanding happened betwixt her parents and herself; the consequence of which was, she took a room by the Common, to follow the business of a mantua-maker, to which she has served an apprenticeship, and could get a good livelihood by it. She gave me an invitation thither to see her as often as I pleased, which happened but seldom, on account of my great distance from it; though this was sufficient to keep our courtship alive.

But my watchful guardian, Mr. Dawkins, for so I may call him, discovered that we continued our intimacy; at which he seemed much displeased; and was astonished that I could not penetrate into her real character, nor see my own folly (as he thought) in persevering in such an inconsiderate proceeding; for it must be confessed, he wished me as well as if I had been a child of his own: so that he could not forbear speaking, when he plainly saw (as he imagined) the trouble I was bringing on myself. But I knew myself to be clear of these things; nevertheless, ought to return Mr. Dawkins thanks for his care over me, since he always supposed me to be a man.

I shall now return to my master and mistress. This pretended or nominal wife had greatly run him in debt for liquor. At a certain time, my master had occasion to go to Gosport; and she resolved to follow him thither. When they both got there, they began to quarrel, and had high words with one another: whereupon he left her, and came home.

As soon as he returned to his house, he shut the front windows, fastened the doors, took the little boy into the room, and caused him to pull off his cloaths, which induced the poor boy to think he was going to flog him: he then ordered the boy to put his two thumbs upon the table, which when he had done, my master put his two thumbs upon the boy's, and compelled him to declare truly, Who had been to see his aunt, and what liquor she had had; for, said he, if you don't tell me truth, I will flog you as long as

I am able. The poor boy dreading the worst, confessed there had been a gentleman to see his aunt, who had a bowl of punch; that she had some beer and brandy for herself; and that whenever any person came to see her, she would send him off for such sorts of liquor as best suited their palate. On which confession he was very well pleased; and directed the boy, with some visible marks of satisfaction, to put on his cloaths.

My master had no sooner opened the door and windows than his wife came in; but he took no notice of any thing at that time. A day or two afterwards, he went to pay Mr. Lambeth for the liquor; then went home and called her to account, enquiring what she had done with so much liquor.

A short time after this, a more disagreeable circumstance than the above happened, which put us all to a stand, and is as follows: My master having occasion to go upon some business to Gosport market, was arrested, carried to a spunging-house, and confined there the whole night. As soon as I was acquainted with the affair, I was determined (in company of my fellow-servant) to go and see him. When we found the house, I enquired if Mr. M'Clean was there? and was answered, Yes. After telling them my business, and who I was, the officer's servant took us up stairs, where we found him in a lock-up-room. But on seeing him in such a place, I could not forbear crying. Whereupon he asked what I cried for? Telling him my reasons, he bid us make ourselves easy, for that he believed to-morrow he should be out; and then caused us both to sit down and refresh ourselves.

After this we returned home, went to bed, and in the morning got up to our work; when we found by the discourse of one of our company, that he had seen my master going to Winchester jail that morning in a post-chaise.

Next morning I set off for Winchester; but did not know one step of the road beyond Farnham; at which place, I was obliged to enquire what road to take. And indeed I thought I never should get there, the passengers being so few to that place; and so much up and down hill, that I could not see Winchester till I came almost into it. It is fifty miles there and back, which I walked in one day.

I soon found out the jail; and having made my errand known, with the reasons for my coming, and a multiplicity of other questions that were asked me, at length the turnkey let me in. But when I saw the felons with their chains on, it much grieved me, to think that my master must stay in such a place. However, I followed the turnkey, who led me from one room to another, till at last he brought me to my master; but could scarce believe his own eyes: nor could I refrain from crying the very instant I saw him; who to moderate my grief, he assured me he should be out again in a little time. But why, says he, do you keep crying? Sir, returned I, to see you in such a place as this. He replied, There are a great many more in this place. Yes, Sir; but you are not like them. Why not like them? Said he. Because, Sir, they are put in for robbing, but you are not.

When I came home, I found my fellow-servant and the little boy together. After I had related to them what I thought proper, we went to bed; and in the morning went to work as usual. However, very fortunately for my fellow-servant and myself, there was one Mr. Colman in the dock-yard, who kept a cabbin for the shipwrights. He being very lame, always carried his chips home in his boat; and if his boys did not come down to carry them, which sometimes they neglected to do, he used to prevail on me to carry them to his house, and would often make me stay supper; and sometimes ordered my fellow-servant to go along with me, where we were sure of being well satisfied, and sent home contentedly; for Mr. Lambert at this time had refused to let us have any farther credit, which in truth put us often into great freights.

At length my mistress came home, and immediately began stripping the house; and carrying the furniture to the pawnbroker's; which indeed was the only method that could be taken to procure us some victuals: and I am sure we had little enough from her; but our neighbours kindness supplied the deficiency. My master was so much in debt that we could not expect any money from him; therefore we were obliged to shift, and live as well as we could. My mistress seldom lay at home above a night in the week, and went abroad in the morning: so that for the remaining part of the week, when I came home from work at night, was obliged to go from house to house as it were in my master's name, or rather on his account, which was upon the whole a very fatiguing situation to me.

It happened once when my mistress was not at home, that I lay in her bed; and Mr. Colman, who was obliged to pass by our door to the waterside, always gave me a call, upon which I jumped out of bed, and told him from the window that I was coming; which occasioned him to spread a report all over the yard, that I was abed with my mistress, because I had looked out of her window; and this they believed was true, (though they did not blame me for it) and the more so because she would frequently come into the yard, and take me with her over to Gosport into those lewd houses in South-street, where I was obliged to be very free with the girls, and where I was promised first to have the daughter of one, and then of another for my wife; so that I had plenty of sweethearts in a little time; and got myself a fine name among them. As I was frequently walking out with some of them, the men of the yard concluded that I was a very amorous spark when in the company of women.

My master still continued in jail; and I did not know when he would be able to get out. It happened however, that the Africa was ordered to sea, the carpenter of which keeping a pawnbroker's shop at Gosport, did not care to go with her; and well knowing what unhappy circumstances my master was in, and that both their ships were of the same rate, thought he would be glad to go in his room, rather than lie in a jail: he therefore wrote a letter, which I was appointed to carry. This office I undertook very readily.

When my master had read the letter, he objected to the proposal in it; as he chiefly wanted all his creditors to agree to a composition, in order for his enlargement. But this the plaintiff refused to consent to, insisting on the whole of the debt being paid, which it was not in his power to do; and he could have willingly turned me over to him as a satisfaction for the debt. But the creditor wanted some-body to pay the money down at once, or to receive all my wages till the whole was paid. My master, however, would not consent to this, unless he would take me altogether, and receive my money from one pay-day to another, as he could think of no other way of discharging the debt. But this Mr. ___ not agreeing to, I set out for home again.

Soon after this, my mistress, as I used to call her, came to me in the yard, and desired that I would come to her at the sign of the Coach and Horses. Accordingly at night, when I left off work, I went and enquired for her at the place where she had directed me; and after meeting with her there, she asked me if I would go to the play with her, and a young woman called Sarah How, who indeed was a very handsome girl. If you will go with us, said she, I will give you a ticket. I promised to her I would go; and from that time the above Sarah How became very free and intimate with me; nor did I ever go to town without calling to see her, when we walked out together; and my mistress believed she had helped me to very agreeable company.

However, the night I went to the play, my mistress took care to be there; and when I came back I was to lie at Mrs. Cook's; but how, and in what manner, I did not yet know. On asking them therefore, where I was to lie? they answered, that I must lie along with them; for they had but one bed, and there were no less than four to lie in it; but it happened to be a very large one. They made me get into the bed first, which I did with my breeches on: but indeed I never had such an uneasy night's lodging before in my life; for they pinched me black and blue; and glad was I at the appearance of morning, when I got up and went to work. But if any body had assured me there were such women existing, I could not have believed it: but God forbid there should be many such!

About this time Mr. Simmons sent for me to come to him directly; and purport of the whole message was, that he had agreed to pay the jail fees to set my master at liberty. My mistress being returned, and present at the time, when she saw Mrs. Simmons give me half a guinea to hire a horse and set off, took it out of my hand, and went to the Dolphin in North-street, Gosport, and there procured a horse to carry us both, though it was not intended she should go, yet being determined upon it, the horse was got ready, and away we set off Jehu-Dobbin-like.

I drove on pretty fast all the way, which occasioned my mistress's cloaths to become quite loose about her; and going through Waltham, the people took me to be a sailor, and that I had got my Moll (as they term them) with me; for her cloaths were almost off.

At last we reached Winchester, about nine o'clock at night; but too late to be admitted into the jail. Next morning being Sunday, my master could get no business done; I was therefore obliged to return back; and in the afternoon about seven o'clock, set off from Winchester, and rode very easy home; but had not gone far before I overtook a young woman whom I invited to ride, (well knowing what fatigue there was in walking). She at first refused my offer. I then asked her how far she had to go? She replied, As far as Waltham. I told her she had better get up and ride. A gate being near, accordingly she got up, and we rode very gently.

She began to ask me where I came from? I replied, From Gosport. At which she laughed, and, said, What! you come from Gosport! Whereupon I repeated to her, That I really did; and added, that if I might be so bold, should be glad to know the reason for asking me such a question? Her answer was, That she had heard great talk of Portsmouth and Gosport, and of the young men and maids there. I said, I hoped she had heard nothing bad of them. Why, returned she, I can't say that I have heard any thing bad of them; but have often heard that the young women are too apt to be seduced. Supposing they are, said I, I hope you will not condemn all for a few. No, says she, I dare affirm there is a mixture of good and bad; God forbid they should be all alike! In this manner we kept talking till we came to Waltham, where she alighted, thanking me for the obliging favour I had done her in giving her a lift.

I soon got safe home; and went to the dockyard to my work as usual. At length the man that arrested my master agreed to have me turned over to him; and Mr. Simmons obtained a board order from my master and him to exchange warrants. This being done, my master made over all his goods to Mr. Simmons; and after they were appraised, he went over to Winchester, paid all the jail fees, and brought my master home with him to Gosport, who soon after went on board the Africa at Spithead, where I went to see him; and he was, I believe, very well pleased with my visit.

Here he began to recount to me what measures he had taken to procure his enlargement; and that as he was under an absolute necessity of going to sea upon those conditions, he hoped that I would use and comply with every reasonable measure for the satisfaction of us both, till it should please God to give a more favourable turn to his affairs: and, proceeded he, you are now to understand, that I have turned you over to Mr. Aulquier; and as soon as I am gone to sea, you must go to him for board wages, which if he does not think proper to allow, you must then board and lodge with him.

Addressing himself next to Mr. Simmons, who was then present, he said, I hope, Sir, that if William should not like to live with Mr. Aulquier, you will be so good as to take him away, and get him board wages. To which Mr. Simmons replied, Yes, Mr. M'Clean, you may depend upon it I will.

Matters being thus agreed upon, Mr. Simmons and I went on shore; but I was to return on board the same evening with my master's watch, and some sea stores: however, there being some difficulty in procuring them that night, I was obliged to defer it till next day; and I lay for that time with this boy, who belonged to the same company as I did. His name was John L___l___y. He was a very sober youth; and well respected by his master and mistress.

I must now return, and proceed to relate how matters went with myself. My master was now gone to sea; and I scarce knew what steps to take; however; one Mr. B___t, cook of the Royal William, told me in a very friendly manner, that he would go along with me to Mr. Aulquier's house. I had never seen him but once before in my life, and that was when he kept the sign of the Bell, before he lived at Kingston, about a mile and a half from the Common, where my master had treated my mistress with a pint of wine. I thought upon the whole I liked him very well. He was, with respect to his person, a handsome man; and was bred a shipwright in Portsmouth yard.

It was now in the year 1765 when this Mr Bout went along with me to Mr. Aulquier's house. We enquired whether he was at home? To which they answered, No; but that he was expected in a short time. However, we went in; and soon after, Mr. Aulquier's wife came from the garden. I really thought she was the handsomest woman I ever saw; but her looking so much younger than he, occasioned me to think that it was impossible she could be his wife.

But to come nearer to the purpose. When Mr. Aulquier came in, I told him my master was gone to sea, and that I had no place to reside in, where I might be maintained; and that it was impossible to work without the convenient necessaries of life. He replied, I am very sensible of that; adding withal, that he did not agree to board me, because my master was to do it. To which I answered, Sir, it is by Mr. Simmons's order I come to you. Well, says he, I shall not give you any board wages; but you may come and board here. Accordingly at night I went to his house; and had not been there long before supper was ordered, which was pork and apple-pudding. When he sat down to his meal, I found I had enough to do to look at him; for he eat in such a voracious manner, that I thought he was going to disgorge it back again upon his plate. He had a brother that lived with him as a servant, to look after his horse, work in the garden, and go on errands, who supped with me when they had done, and whom I was to lay with. In the morning

I went to work in the dock as usual; and was put to the inconvenience of walking a mile backwards and forwards to and from dinner, being only allowed an hour and half for that purpose, which was very disagreeable to me.

Having thus agreed with my new master, the first thing he set me to do was to clean his shoes, knives, and forks, every night, which being a slavish and dirty employment, wore out everything I had on my back. This sort of business I had to do after my work in the yard, before I went to bed.

It may with great truth be said, that Mr. A__'s house entertained a very bad set of people: I had not been long with him before he turned me over to another man to pay his debts; and when I had worked that out, was again turned over to a third: so that being shifted from one to another, I had neither cloaths to my back, nor shoes or stockings to my feet; notwithstanding which, I was frequently (even in the dead of winter) obliged to go to the dock-yard bare-footed.

But my hardships did not end here; for the little provision I sometimes had, would scarce enable me to go through the work of the yard; and sometimes I had none at all. And to add to my farther miseries, as though I had not enough already, they compelled me to lay with the most vile and abandoned wretches of all denominations, who were in all respects the greatest blackguards that ever could be seen: so that for five years and a half of my apprenticeship I went through as great a variety of hardships as any person in my station could possibly experience.

One evening after my work at the dock-yard, though in very rainy weather, I was sent with the cart to the Common to fetch grains, which made me very wet. But as they seemed to pay very little regard to my condition, I took a candle, and went up stairs to bed; and was scarce there before I heard all the house in an uproar, the cause of which I could not immediately learn. Soon after this, I heard my master calling his wife Lewis's whore, and her mother a bitch, which caused me to make some reflection on what the young man had told me before.

At this time there was a young woman that had been a servant there three years, and knew their temper very well. This person, as soon as the noise and quarrel was over, began to think of me. She accordingly came up, and brought with her a pint of beer, and some bread and cheese, telling me not to mind their quarrels, for it was no new thing, as it very often happened. I thought within myself, they may quarrel as often as they please, for I should never quarrel with them. Next day when I came home, and the storm was over, there was nothing heard but my dear; and they appeared as loving as if no quarrel had ever happened.

Not long after this, on my coming home to dinner, I found my mistress throwing all the maid's cloaths out of the chamber window, at the same time calling her all the abusive names she could think of, which set the poor maid a crying, almost ready to break her heart; all which gave me great concern; the poor woman making no other request than only desiring her wages might be paid, that she might go about her business. But when I came home at night, I found things bore a different face; for all was made up, and every thing appeared quite calm: and she promised, that as soon as they removed to Gosport, she should be their chambermaid.

It being now brought to my mind, that I continued very undutiful in not having writ to my father and mother for some considerable time, I therefore took this opportunity of so doing; and shall here present the reader with the letter, which is as follows:

Kingston, Dec. 5 1765.

"Hond. Father and Mother

"This comes with my duty to you both, hoping these few lines will find you in

good health, as I am at present, though I live
but very poorly. My master, after having been
in gaol some time for debt, in order to regain his
liberty, was obliged to go to sea, before which
he turned me over to one Mr. Aulquier. He
is not so kind to me as my old master was,
whose return home I will endeavour to wait for
with patience, though that will not be these
three years; nevertheless, I still hope I shall
see him again: for he behaved towards me more
like a father than a master. I hope my brother
and sisters are well, and all friends that know
me; and I beg you will write as soon as it suits
you, to let me know how you both are. I
conclude with praying for the blessing of God
to attend you both, from

"Your most undutiful daughter,
"MARY LACY."

These were the contents of the letter that I sent to my
father and mother. I must now return to my former narrative; and inform you, that as the maid was to stay again,
she and I one day began to talk about sweethearts. I told
her there was a young woman I kept company with, who

lived upon the Common; but that Mr. Dawkins had persuaded me to break off my acquaintance with her. I then observed, that she was a very pretty girl; and, when I lived at Kingston, she would often come to the dock-yard to see me, and we sometimes walked over the Common together, and one of us afterwards accompanied the other home alternately. It happened when we had been a pretty long time in each other's company, that I had scarce reached home, and taken care of the horse, before it was time to go to bed; so that I thought myself in a critical situation, because she often declared, as I have before observed, that she would stay twelve years for me, if I would promise to marry her.

Christmas-Day being now come, we all went to live at Gosport, which was the more agreeable to me, as I had some time to eat my dinner; and, being made boatswain of the dock-boat, I had a shilling a week for the locking up and care of her, which was a great benefit to me, though the money was earned with great labour and fatigue; for let the weather be ever so unfavourable, I was obliged to be with her.

My master and I now agreed very well; but I did not like my new bedfellow, as he was a young man that attended the billiard table, yet of an exceeding good temper, but one that loved the women, though a little inconstant; which made me very uneasy in my mind, for fear he should find me out.

One night when I came home, there were many compliments passed betwixt us; for as I observed before, he was thoroughly good natured: so that if I wanted any thing that he could get, I was sure to have it. But there was one thing I greatly disliked in him; and that was, when he came to bed, he was extremely talkative, and made a very great noise, which broke my rest. However, notwithstanding this, nobody could come into my room but I heard them; and therefore thought myself obliged to pass over this circumstance as well as I could, though the best of it was disagreeable enough.

I must take occasion to mention here, that being now pretty well settled in our house, my master bought a four-oar'd boat, which we put in one of the coach houses, and shoar'd her up; so that when I left the yard at night, I went to work upon her.

I shall now leave my master and bedfellow, and return to my old sweetheart, who still lived on the Common. On Shrove-Tuesday, in the year 1766, one of her brothers came and asked me if I would go to his sister's house, as there was to be dancing there. I went accordingly the same day;

but though I was ignorant of dancing, yet I thought my going might induce her to think more of me. When we came to the place, she asked me why I did not care to dance? I told her the reason (the fame which I formerly mentioned) that if I once began to revel and dance, I should not easily leave it off; that it would inevitably lead me into bad company, and render me incapable of doing my duty in the yard; all which I supposed would be sufficient to make her desist from importuning me any more on that head; and that my not going near her, would be a sure means of making her forget me. However, I found myself mistaken; for one day, as I was going down the Common in Union-street, she happened to stand at a door; and seeing me, said, Will, I thought you was dead. Why so? returned I; did you send any body to kill me? No, replied she; but I thought I should never see you any more. What made you think so? You know the reason well enough. Well, said I, you are welcome to think so still, if you please; but I must be going. What! said she, you are in a great hurry now to be gone; if you was along with that Gosport girl you would not be in such haste to leave her. I said, I am not in such a hurry to be gone from your company, Betsy; what makes you think so? After this little chat, though with some seeming reserve on both sides, she asked if I would come in? I went in and sat down, and then asked her if she would come next Sunday to Gosport, and drink tea? She told me she would. Thus it was all made up again.

When Sunday came, I went down to wait the boat's coming, to help her out, which was just before my master's house, where all the servants were looking at me, and at my girl; but I paid no regard to that.

From this place we went to my old mistress, who was to make tea for us. The old gentlewoman was highly pleased to think she had met with one who was formerly her man, in company with his sweetheart, to drink tea with her. She told the young woman, I was a clever little man, and that I would make a very good husband. After tea, miss and I walked out; and then I went over the water to see her safe home.

On my coming home in the evening, all the servants asked me how my spouse did? I told them she was in good health. This occasioned Sarah to be a little jocose on me about it; however, it passed on. But, by some means or other, Mr. Dawkins had heard we kept company again; on which he was very angry with me. In order to pacify him, I went down to his house, when he immediately asked me how Miss Betsy did? How does Miss Betsy do! said I; upon my word, Sir, I don't know. Not know! said he; when you go on the Common, and call in to see her! when you are so great, and walk out together! William, I am sorry you will walk out with her, when I have told you what she is. Well, Sir, said I, I am much obliged to you for your advice; but as for keeping her company, I do not; nor do I know that I shall ever speak to her again.

This matter passed over for some time; and by giving attention to my work, I thought little or nothing about things of this kind. However, one evening my fellow-servant, Sarah Chase, began talking as we were sitting together about sweethearts, and said to me in a joking manner, I think you have lost your intended. Well, I replied, I must be content. She said, There are more in the world to be had. Ay, replied I, when one is gone, another will come. For my part, added she, I have got never a one. Why, returned I, I think, Sarah, you are joking with me now; are you not? No, said she, I am not; observing at the same time, that she thought we were both in one condition. Well, said I, suppose you and I were to keep company together? You and I, answered she, will consider of it.

I had not yet served quite three years of my time; nevertheless, it was agreed upon to keep company together; and that neither of us should walk out with any other person, without the mutual consent of each other. Notwithstanding this agreement, if she saw me talking to any young woman, she was immediately fired with jealousy, and could scarce command her temper. This I did sometimes to try her. However, we were very intimate together. And to give me a farther proof of her affection, she would frequently come down to the place where the boat landed, to see me, which made the people believe we should soon be married. One observed to me, Well done, Chandler, you come on very well: another, that she and I do it very well: and then a third would add, that I should be a cuckold before I had long been married, for that she was too large for me, and I should make but a little man; and many such like ridiculous remarks.

This young woman was always very fond of walking out with me, where we were sure of meeting with some of the shipwrights, which I well knew I should hear of the next day I went to work; when they began rallying afresh. Ay, ay, Chandler thinks himself as fine a man as any of them, now he has got a sweetheart; let him go on, he will soon have a child sworn to him. Ay, ay, says another, this is not the first he has had, for he had one on the Common; but I heard that a sailor ran away with her; however, Chandler has found a comely one in her room: and when they saw us together remarked, Ay, ay, there goes a woman and her husband.

Notwithstanding these things, it soon came to pass that Sarah began to have a very suspicious opinion of me, on observing I spoke to another girl; for one evening when I went in doors to ask her for some supper, she looked at me with a countenance that bespoke a mixture of jealousy and anger. It then came into my mind, that there would soon be terrible work. Whereupon I asked what was the matter with her? She told me to go to the squint-ey'd girl, and enquire the matter there. Very well, said I, so I can; from hence I soon knew what was the ground of all.

It seems the tap-house woman had been telling her more of this affair at large, which brought me into a great difficulty; and indeed I lived a very disagreeable life, at home especially; since I could not get my victuals as before. On which account, I went and asked the cook what was the matter with Sarah? She said, I knew very well what ailed her. Well, replied I, she will come again very soon; during which time, when I was at home, there was nothing but grumbling. Sarah declared at the same time, that she would never speak to me again; pretending too that she did not want for a companion, which she thought would vex me, though I well knew she had none. However, to make some amends for this, the young woman sent me a letter, the contents of which are as follow.

"Sir,   *April, 26, 1766.*

"This comes with my kind love to you,
hoping these few lines will find you in
good health, as I am at present; and shall take
it as a favour, if, dear Mr Chandler, you will
give me the pleasure of your company this
evening; for you are so agreeable, that I don't
know how to be without you: and if you can't
come, I shall be very uneasy about you; for
without you I am quite unahappy. So no more
at present, from

"From your sincere Lover,
"E.W."

When I had read this letter, I could not help laughing heartily. But I was apprehensive that the woman of the tap-house would come and tell Sarah that the letter was from this young woman; therefore I did not answer it, because I could pretend it was on account of Sarah's using me so ill; for she thought she could do with me as she pleased. Knowing therefore her attachment to me, I used to place myself at a window where I saw this young woman pass and repass in quest of me: for she could not think where I was; which induced her to watch my bedfellow, and ask him if I was not well? But he thought I was deeply in love with Sarah.

These circumstances made me seriously reflect what troubles I had brought on myself: so that by running over one thing after another, and nobody to relate my tale to, of the trouble and sorrow I had brought upon my parents, and the hardship I was like to endure myself; I say these things crowding in upon me at once, worked on my spirits at particular times to such a degree, that they robbed me of all my peace: and if at any time I endeavoured to give vent to these melancholy reflections, my expressions of grief were immediately ridiculed as the effects of love. And they would sometimes tell Sarah, that I had been crying all night for her; adding, How can you slight him so! Not I indeed, said she; it is all his own fault; for if he had not refused me, I should not him. And glad I was that she appeared so indifferent; for they little knew the cause of my troubles.

In this and such like manner things went on for four or five weeks, during which time I had not seen the young woman. For as I had kept myself close within doors, she had no opportunity of seeing me. She therefore determined to write me another letter, and leave it with the woman of the tap-house, which she accordingly did; and at night the woman brought it to me; of which the following is a copy for the perusal of the reader.

"Dear SIR,

"This comes with my kind love to you, hoping these few lines will find you in good health; but I cannot say the same; because I am full of trouble, to think you slight my company. But I don't wonder at it; as I find you have so much love for Sarah. I know you can't love us both; and since it is your choice, I hope you will marry her, and spend your days together in pleasure. But though it is not my lot to have you, yet I hope you will be kind enough to answer this letter; or, if you will come and speak to me, I shall take it as a great favour, and that is all I can desire of you. So no more at present, from

"Your sincere Lover,

"E.W."

When I had read the above letter, I was resolved to go and hear what she had to say. Accordingly I went: but as soon as she saw me, she fell a laughing. Upon which I told her, I should be glad to know what she wanted with me? Hereupon she said, She thought I slighted her, by keeping company with Sarah; but now, added she, those thoughts all vanish, for I knew your intimacy with her would not continue long. How came you to think so: said I: was it that I might keep you company? Why, said she, when I sent you the first letter, desiring to see you, you came; which was a very sufficient reason for me to think you would comply with my request. To this I replied, I am sensible that I came at your desire, but was wholly ignorant of your intentions, or that your inclinations tended to me; for I urged, you must consider how long I have to serve of my time. She answered, I don't want to be married yet, if you will only consent to keep me company. Pray, returned I, what good will that do you, since you are not over hasty to be married? Well, says she, to put an end to this matter, since you seem to slight me, I will go and live in the country. To which I answered, I did not slight her at all; and to bid her a good night; and home I went.

As soon as I came into the house I was set upon by Sarah; and in short, there was not any place I could go to but I was pointed at some way or other, whether at work or elsewhere; for I was looked upon as a smart fellow among the women; all which only increased Sarah's pain, by reason of my keeping this girl's company.

When I went to bed, my bedfellow said to me, Chandler, if ever you speak to Sarah again, you deserve to have your head cut off. On which I told him, that I should not speak to her again for some time. Indeed he was frequently speaking to me about her; and frankly told me it would be my ruin, if I did not take care of myself: for, says he, you look dull very often, tho' I knew it was not upon her account, but merely owing to my own foolishness.

It was now in the year 1767, when I came to a resolution to see my father and mother; and obtained leave for that purpose, as the navy had orders at that time to sail for the Downs the first fair wind. They sailed on the Sunday, and we got thither on Monday, when I went on shore, and afterwards passed on to Deal, where I breakfasted. After dinner I set off for Sandwich, where I had some letters to deliver; which having done, I set forward for Ash. When I came there, I went thro' the church-yard, and read the head-stones, and saw several people I knew, though they did not recollect me. However, having a letter to deliver from a young woman to her aunt, who once knew me very well, though she had now almost forgot me, she read it; and looking at me with a mixture of surprise and joy, said, I will be whipped if you are not Mary Lacy. This expression of her's forced a flood of tears from me; for indeed she was very glad to see me.

I had not yet seen my mother; and the above woman was extremely solicitous as well as myself to manage our interview with a suitable precaution; left from too great transport of joy, some bad consequence might happen, which very often does, in such extraordinary cases. However, it was agreed, that I should stay in another room till she had opened the matter, and prepared my mother to receive me. In a short time after, she came and told me not to be uneasy. But I could not forbear crying, being under apprehensions of my mother's fainting. She came in a little time afterwards, and ran to embrace me with all the transport and affection of a tender mother, saying, O, my dear child, where have you been all this time from me, that I could not see you before! After mutual and affectionate salutations, we went home, where I soon found all the family very well; and took this opportunity of satisfying their earnest expectations, by recounting the various turns of fortune I had met with and gone thro', during my absence for almost eight years.

Before I quit this matter, it should be observed, the young man on whose account I at first left my parents, had frequently caused enquiry to be made when I was to come home, expressing a great desire to see me: but I had no inclination to receive any visits from him. And having now been at home nine days, I signified my desire of leaving them, which caused them to shed many tears. It was now Thursday; and my time expired on the Sunday following, when, pursuant to my leave of absence, I was to be at Portsmouth.

At length, after parting from my friends, I set off, and came first to Canterbury, and soon afterwards reached Chatham by the help of a coach, where I expected to lie that night; but learning that another coach was going to London, I watched an opportunity of getting a lift in it; thinking that if I could get there at night, I should be able to reach Portsmouth in good time on Sunday. But I had not gone far behind the coach before the guide's light went out: however, he went and lighted it again; and when he returned with it, seeing me behind, he made me get down, though I told him I would pay him for it.

It now rained hard, which made me very wet; and the night being quite dark, I did not know where I was: so that in this dreary condition I had no prospect of a house to shelter myself from the inclemency of the weather. But being still inclinable to trudge on, I at length, though unexpectedly, found myself at Gravesend, where I had some refreshment. The people of the house where I had a little repast, on hearing me say that I wanted to go to London in the morning, told me I might go in one of the boats at six o'clock. I paid for my lodging and supper before I went to bed, and desired them to call me up in the morning. Accordingly I went on board; but the wind being unfavourable, we were much longer than usual in getting up to London.

Among the passengers on board this boat there was one old lady, who took me to be sea-faring man, and enquired where I came from? I told her, From Gosport. From Gosport! said she; who do you live with there, pray? I answered her, With one Mr. Aulquier. She replied, I don't know him; but asked me if I was acquainted with one Mrs. ___? Yes, ma'am, returned I, I know her well; for my mistress and she are very intimate. Why, returned this old procuress, she is my daughter. At which I gave a dry look, and thought to myself she was a dextrous hand at a watch. She then asked me to take a glass of wine, and a bit of cake, which I accepted, as I knew it would do me good; and at the same time asked if I would (when they got to London) carry a little box to her daughter that lived just at hand, telling me at the same time, she would shew me London, and put me in the road to Kingston; all which I did: and when I came to the door, which her supposed daughter opened, there immediately came down stairs and addressed me as fine a girl as ever my eyes beheld, who at first sight I knew must be a kept mistress. To say the truth, this old Duenna regaled me very handsomely; and afterwards set out for the Royal Exchange, and to see other curiosities. In this walk (which was a very extensive one) I luckily met with a carpenter of a ship, who knew me very well, and asked me where I was going? I told him to Portsmouth. Why says he, this is the wrong way; I am going down, and you may as well go with me. Accordingly we set off: but he stopping to speak to a person, I left him, and travelled on by myself. Soon afterwards he overtook me at Leephook, where hearing me talk, he knew my voice, called to me, and said, What, Chandler, are you got so far already! Yes, Sir, said I; but I am almost tired, and don't care to go any farther to-night. No more will I, said he: but where did you lie last night? Why, Sir, I lay at Kingston. So did I, replied he, and endeavoured to find you out, but could not; and what did you pay for your lodging? Sixpence, Sir, returned I. If you had been along with me, said he, you might have had one for twopence. We then went to a house and got a beef steak, etc. for supper, and lay there; and the whole expence amounted only to sixteen pence. On asking him what I had to pay, he said, Nothing. But before we went to bed, the landlady asked if we lay together? Yes, said he, my friend Chandler is a clean lad. He little knew who he had got to lie with him; I am sure if he had, I should have been otherwise disposed in this respect; for he was always too free among the women.

In the morning we set off, and some time afterwards stopt to refresh ourselves; but he would not suffer me to pay any thing: so that I thought I lived very cheap. Though I was lame, and greatly fatigued by this journey, nevertheless I made shift to get to Portsmouth punctually at the time appointed, and soon crossed the water to Gosport.

As soon as I was come to my master's house, my mistress, being in a good humour, gave me some refreshment immediately; and I then told her I had seen Mrs. Cureall's mother at London, and of the civility she shewed me at home and abroad. Whereupon my mistress sent for her; and we had a great deal of conversation together. At night I went to bed, and slept very sound.

In the morning I went to work as usual. But on my return home at night, my mistress was standing at the bar, and Mrs. Cureall with her. Seeing me come in, she said to Mrs. Cureall, here comes my little curl-pou'd dog; he is ashamed to come and kiss me; and I can't say but what I was. Upon this I went backwards to consider how I should act, provided she should say so again. After having considered how I should behave myself on this occasion, I went in; and the very moment she saw me return, said, Why I told you he was ashamed to come and kiss me. No, that I am not, said I. Accordingly I went to her; and she stooped down to let me kiss her, when I perceived she was very much in liquor; so that I was obliged to put her to bed, our maid being abed with a young man, who swore next morning that I had been in bed with my mistress. Indeed as I was willing to do any thing for a quiet life, it was no wonder that such reports prevailed among the people; though they all agreed that I acted quite right.

But I must here acknowledge with truth, that the frequent quarrels and fighting between my master and mistress made my life very uncomfortable. Their differences and skirmishes were so often repeated, that I was obliged to take a tinderbox in my room to strike a light upon occasion, and go down to part them if I could. One night it happened that I forgot the box; but was obliged to leave my bed on their account, though without light. In groping my way without cloaths on in the street, I stumbled upon a door that was ajar, where I perceived the glimmering of a candle upon the mantle-piece, which I was going to take, not thinking any person was near; when on a sudden a woman entered the room, and cried out, What the devil do you do here naked! I begged of her not to stop me, because I was in a hurry: and have often since thought it was a great mercy I was not found out, that being a very bad house: and it was still a greater wonder that the woman did not take hold of me.

I had no sooner got within doors than I found my mistress with her head out of the window, crying, Murder, as loud as she could bawl, with the children all in tears about her; which frightened me very much, my master appealing to me as a witness if he was beating her; for he lay at the same time in his bed laughing at her. When she was grown tired on this howling fit, I asked her if she would go to bed, and not alarm the people by these uproars? On which, she said, O the dog! I'll pull out his guts! Come, said I, will you go to some other bed, and take no father notice of him to-night? But it was all to no purpose; since the more I talked to her the worse she was, and the greater noise she made. At length, I got her up stairs, and put her into another bed, where she lay pretty quiet till the morning.

I was indeed very glad when the morning came, that I might go to the dock to my work, because there I was free from noise. However, the men used to tell me, out of a sort of waggery, that they would have my mistress and me taken up for common disturbers. I wish you would, said I, for then I should have some peace.

Some time after this, when I came home at night from the dock-yard, I found the maid was going away; and my master being gone over the water, my mistress, who was pretty much intoxicated, put on her hat and cloak, and would forsooth cross the water to find him, which she did at the sign of the Fountain in Portsmouth. The first salute she generally gave him, was a great blow with the first thing she could meet with; which put him into such a passion, that he rose up and beat her in such a violent manner with a stick, that he left her almost lifeless.

Soon after this fray, my mistress came home, where she found me reading my book, and rocking the cradle. On observing her countenance, I perceived she had two black eyes; so that I immediately concluded she had been after my master for something. She then asked me if he was come home? I told her, No. Whereupon she loaded him with the most reproachful names her imagination could suggest; and afterwards went abroad again.

She had not been gone long before my master came home, and asked if my mistress was come? I told him, She had been at home, but was gone. Whereupon he took a candle, hammer, and nails, went up to his bedchamber, and nailed the door up, to prevent her coming to bed to him.

He had not been in bed long before she came back; and then I apprehended I should have no sleep that night; for I found the old trade was going on again. She asked, If my master was come in? I answered, Yes. O the dog! said she,

I'll pull him out of his bed; for he shall have no rest here this night; and up stairs she flew. But finding the door was fast, she came down immediately in a great fury for something to break it open, but met with nothing, as I had taken care to put every thing out of her reach; for she would take the first thing that came to hand. By some means or other she at length got a scrubbing brush, with which she soon broke a piece out of the door, and then sat down looking through it, saying, Now I can see you, I am content. But she had not sat long before she got up and fell to work again, till she had demolished the door so far as to make room enough to go in herself; but was afraid to sit down. Having thus done, she went and brought up the young child; and getting upon her knees, first put the child in at the door, and afterwards entered herself. This being done, she threw the child (which was only about two months old) at him: so that I was very much afraid she had killed it. I ran down to fetch the cradle to put the child in, and there sat till three o'clock; all which time they continued fighting; sometimes one getting the better, and sometimes the other; during the whole of which encounter I was obliged to see fair play, though murder should be the consequence. These contests frequently happened, till it was time for me to go to work; and I was very glad to be out of their way; besides, the children were ever crying after me:

and it gave me great concern to think the mother should have so little regard for her family, as to neglect them in the manner she did. However, I have some reason to believe the fault was equally chargeable on the husband.

Though I was not turned over to another master, I could not get quite clear of my former; for when I came from the dock, my mistress would make me clean shoes, knives and forks, and do all the drudgery of the house as before. But I had sometimes the courage to tell her, that I was not put 'prentice to be treated in such a manner: with that she catched me by the hair of the head, and turned me out of doors; which the people observing, asked if she was not ashamed to use me in such a rough manner? She said, I should not come there again; though it was excessive cold weather, and I had no friend to go to. Upon this, I went to the taphouse at the Red Lyon, and told the woman in what manner my mistress had served me, and that I would not go there any more if I could help it, though I had no money to pay for a lodging. The woman then told me I should lay there.

On going to work next day, I told the men in the yard in what manner I had been handled by my mistress. They bid me go to the man that I was turned over to, and ask him for my board wages, he being (they said) the only fit person to apply to. Next day I went and told him my case.

Whereupon he directed me to come the following day, and he would send his brother over to Mr. Aulquier's, which he did. But Mr. Aulquier would not agree to give me board wages; saying, That if I would not come home and board, he would do nothing more for me. During this time I was obliged to shift as well as I could: But my mistress sent all over the town to find me out, in order to get me back again; however, I took care she should not meet with me.

Soon after this, I went to the Common, to see one Mrs. Reading, who knew me very well when I was on board the Sandwich; and asked me in a very friendly manner how I did? I began with telling her how my mistress had served me, by turning me out of doors. She immediately said, You shall live with me, and that she would engage to get my board wages. Hereupon I went over to Gosport, and related the matter to the woman, telling her where I was going to live, and thanked her for my lodging. She said, I was very welcome; for while I lay there I had a sailor for my bedfellow, and I was glad when I parted from him.

After this I returned to the Common, and lay with Mrs. Reading's eldest son, who had no suspicion of my being a woman; and I lived with her as one of her own children; and the man I was turned over to promised me my board wages: on which I thought myself happy.

I shall now present the reader with a letter I sent to my father and mother, as follows:

Gosport, Feb. 2, 1768.
Hond. Father and Mother,

"*This comes with my duty to you both,*
hoping these few lines will find you in
good health, as I am at present, thanks be to
God for it. Your last letter I received very
safe; and am glad to find my mother is so well
recovered. Since I wrote to you, I have been
turned over to another master, one Mr. Bed-
worth, who lives upon the Common. My
kind love to my brother and sister, and all
friends that know me. So conclude with my
duty and prayers for you both, from

   Your dutiful daughter,

   "*MARY LACY,*
"*N.B. Please to direct for me thus,*

"*To William Chandler, at the King of Prussia's*
   "*Head, in Gosport".*

To resume my former narrative. My master being returned home from the king's-bench, they were very solicitous for me to come home again; which I would not consent to till my friend Mrs. Reading was satisfied for my board and lodging, which they promised should be paid, as soon as they received some money due to them from a sailor, who at that time was on the other side the water, in Portsmouth town. In order the more speedily to obtain it, they employed an officer to arrest him. But he being well known, they were afraid to go into the houses to look after him; and therefore came home, and said he could not be found.

My mistress then asked me if I would go with her in search of him (which was to be the night following)? To this I the more readily consented, as I was very desirous my friend should have her money. Accordingly next night we went over to the Naked Boy at Portsmouth, and there found him playing at bowls. My mistress then went up to him, and asked if he would drink? whilst I went to call the bailiff's follower: but before I could return, he decamped. She cried out, Stop thief, with the follower after her: nevertheless, he got clear off for that time.

Soon after, we went in search of him again; and among the number of people we saw, I met with the boatswain's mate of the Sandwich, who stared at me, and asked what brought me out at that time of night? I told him I was looking for a particular person, but could not find him; and asked him if there were any other people in the house? To which he answered, There were some up stairs. I then called the bailiff, went up stairs, and found him in bed with a girl, with his face very bloody. We pulled him out of bed, and carried him to Gosport. Mr. Aulquier was gone to bed; however, we soon obliged him to get up, and secured the person we were in quest of. But, notwithstanding all the pains and fatigue I had been at in this troublesome affair, my poor landlady did not recover any of the money due to her, the man being insolvent.

We began now to live at the same poor rate as heretofore, having sometimes had victuals, and at other times none. At length my master gave me two-pence a day for a dinner; and indeed I could not well have less. However, by some fortunate means or other, I used to procure a dinner; so I reserved that two-pence for other uses.

My Master was now become so poor, that he was not able to buy me a pair of shoes: and tho' at this time it was very cold wet weather, I was obliged to go almost barefooted. However, to make things a little more comfortable, when I went home at night, I used to wash my stockings, and dry them before the fire, to be as comfortable as I could the next day. I had no money to purchase second-hand shoes, which if I had had, they would not have lasted long;

and as for shirts, I was obliged to go on trust for them, till I could pay. But I always took care to discharge what I owed for one thing before I bought another; and that was the way I got my cloaths.

The next day I went to the dock, it was whispered about that I was a woman; which threw me into a most terrible fright, believing that some of the boys were going to search me. It was now much about breakfast-time; when coming on shore, in order to go to my chest for my break-fast, two men of our company called, and said, They wanted to speak to me. I went to them. What think you, Chandler, the people will have it that you are a woman! which struck me with such a panic that I knew not what to say. However, I had the presence of mind to laugh it off, as if it was not worth notice.

On going to my chest again, I perceived several appren-tices waiting, who wanted to search me: but I took care not to run, lest that should increase their suspicion. Hereupon, one Mr. Penny, of our company, came up, and asked them what they meant by surrounding me in that manner? telling them at the same time, that the first person that offered to touch me, he would not only well drub him, but carry him before the builder afterwards, which made them all sheer off; and they were from that time afraid of molesting me any more.

I now sat down, and gave full vent to my tears, which were not few: but the men that I worked with, were gone to breakfast, and knew nothing of the matter till they came back; when my friends thus accosted them, What think you of your man now? Why, 'tis no such thing, said the others, and I'll wager you any money upon it; which made me glad to think they gave it such a turn. However, when I had done work, the man whose name was Corbin, and his mate that taught me my business, came and told me in a serious manner, I must go with them to be searched; for if you don't said they, you will be over-haul'd by the boys. Indeed I knew not what to do in this case: but I considered they were very sober men, and that it was safer to trust them than expose myself to the rudeness of the boys. They put the question very seriously, which I as ingenuously answered, though it made me cry so that I could scarce speak; at which declaration of mine, in plainly telling them I was a woman, they seemed greatly surprised; and offered to take their oaths of secresy.

When they went back, the people asked them if it was true what they had heard? No, said they, he is a man and a half to a great many. Ay, said one, I thought Chandler could not be so great with his mistress if he was not a man; I'm sure she would not have brought him to the point if he was not so: and another said, I'm sure he's no girl; if he was, he would not have gone after so many for nothing, and would have soon been found out. From such talk as this among the men, in a day or two the matter quite dropt: yet now and then they would say, I wonder how it should come into the heads of the people to think that Chandler was a girl: I am sure there is not the least appearance of it in the make or shape of him. Indeed Mr. Corbin never gave the least hint or token of such a suspicion, any more than if he had not known or thought any thing of the matter: nor could I discover or conceive, at the time, what gave rise to this extraordinary affair, or by what means it could take wind about the yard. My girl at Gosport had heard it, but could not believe it. She believed I had received every favour, and taken every freedom that could be practised by the gallants, or she would not have given her company to me, though at this time I was not so very intimate with her as heretofore.

I must now return to my old lady, who was going to remove to another house; so that there was no space for me to lie in, which obliged me to go home to my master's house, who had lately hired a new servant. I was to lie in the fore garret, and she in the back one. Mr. Aulquier lay below; but I had some suspicion they lay together, though I never heard her go up or down stairs. However, when I went down one morning, I overheard them talking, which confirmed me in the opinion that they were bedfellows. It grieved me to think what ruin the girl was bringing upon herself; and therefore thought it my duty to tell her of it, which I did when I came home to dinner, though she denied it: but when I came to tax her with what passed betwixt them, she could not help owning it to me. Whereupon I advised her to leave him. She said, She did not know what to do. And I should have been heartily glad if she had quitted the place; for she used me very ill, by dashing my milk with water at supper, and then charging the fault upon another. And at dinner time, when they had duck, fowl, or any fine roast meat, they would frequently send me away with a piece of bread and cheese, by saying that dinner would not be dressed time enough for me. But she soon afterwards began to use me better, being afraid I should go and inform her mother of her behaviour. The following Sunday Mr. Aulquier and she fell out, and had a scuffle together; and in the fray she tore off his shirtsleeves, and then went out of doors. So that there being nobody to dress the dinner but me, I put on the pot with some pork and greens, which was a good meal for me. But he soon prevailed on her to come back again.

It will be necessary here to make some farther mention of my old mistress, who still lived along with Mr. ___. She took no thought or concern about her children, and was alike neglectful of herself, owing to her turbulent and furious disposition: for after she had lived with Mr. A___r but a short time, she cut his head and hand with a quart pot, which provoked him to send her to Bridewell for her good behaviour. While she was there, her mother desired me to carry a letter to her, which I said I would do, provided she first obtained my master's consent; which he readily granted. Upon bringing her the letter, she said, Bill, what do you think I dreamt of last night? I don't know, said I. Why, says she, I dreamt that you and I were married. O then, replied I, you will have a good husband when you have me. Whereupon she called for a pot of beer, to drink with her: she then read the letter, the contents of which gave her a better opinion of herself; and afterwards asked me if I would go to Mr. Rimes, the man she had lived with, and endeavour to prevail upon him to procure her release. I told her I would, which I accordingly did; when he began with telling in what manner she had used him. Well, said I, you have put her in, and you must take her out again. He replied, I know I must; and this I know also, that all the people will think me an arrant fool for so doing; however, you may let her know, that she shall be discharged to-morrow. I went immediately and told the mother and her what I had done in the matter. The mother was glad to hear of my success in it; but desired (tho' she was her child) that she would not come near her again.

To return to my old sweetheart Sarah. The next day when I was going from work, she came up to the dock-yard, and asked me if I would go along with her to a christening? After a short pause, I told her I did not care to stand for the child. Whereupon she went and gave the people notice of my dislike to the proposal, who took care to provide a godfather in my room. But notwithstanding my refusal to answer for the child, I could not be excused from going with her to the house: so that when I came from the dock after dinner, I was obliged to lose half a day's work to please her. We were very merry together: everything was conduced in tolerable order; and we broke up in good time, which gave me an opportunity of seeing her home; which caused a report to be spread all over the town, that we were going to be married next day; and there were many that believed it. For my part I was glad that I was so near the expiration of my time, because I should then be my own master; for I still went to Mr. L___'s, and met with a very good sort of gentlewoman who lived there. She asked me if I went to church? I told her, Yes, when I had an opportunity. She afterwards gave me many useful admonitions, which disposed me to be very thankful to God for his goodness, in protecting me amidst the many dangers I had brought upon myself: and I flattered myself that I should some time or other be enabled to make amends to my parents for all the trouble I had brought upon them. But the worst embarrassment I had involved myself in, was my being so intimate with Sarah. Indeed I had almost taken a resolution to break off correspondence, not only with Sarah, but even with every one of those with whom I had contracted an acquaintance of that sort; for I found it almost impossible to free myself from their importunities any other way.

I considered it as a very surprizing event that Mrs. L___ should pretend to have such a regard for my interest, and at length betray me. She told me, I should be welcome to come and lodge with her, when I was out of my time; and by continually repeating this profession of her kindness towards me, I thought she was the best friend I had; for I could not form the least idea of her being so deceitful as to discover me, after she had given my mother an absolute promise to the contrary. Indeed I esteemed myself happy in having met with a person I could freely unbosom myself to, being perfectly satisfied of her fidelity; on which account I really thought I could not make her a too grateful return; which consideration often induced me to carry her a bundle of chips.

I shall now proceed to the concluding scenes of my folly. Being but very indifferently accommodated in regard to cloathing, my master aggravated my distress, by not permitting me to receive the three pounds a year; neither would he procure me any apparel, though the money was regularly paid him: and, notwithstanding he enjoyed every advantage he could possibly expect, yet was so unkind as to refuse me even a pair of shoes, when I was barefooted.

On the day before my time expired, being at work upon the Pallas frigate, Sarah came and invited me to breakfast with her the next morning, which I did. Having afterwards cleaned myself, I went to the builder's office, and told him, it was the last day of my time, and hoped he had no objection against my certificate's being allowed me. On asking to whom I served my time? I told him. He then called his clerk, and ordered him to prepare my certificate, which he accordingly did; after which, I went to each of the proper persons, who readily signed it. I then carried the certificate to the clerk of the cheque's office, where I was entered as a man.

After this I went to reside upon the Common, as I supposed it would be most satisfactory to my mother. I lived there as retired as I could, and kept to my work. Soon after which, the company that I belonged to were ordered to go and break up an old ship that lay in the dock: but we found it very hard to demolish her; and I likewise found the labour much too hard for me, tho' I never gave out; for at the best of times the work was very fatiguing. But the money we earned was acceptable to me, since having owed some during my apprenticeship, I was glad to have it in my power to pay every one as fast as I could: and, beside, I was willing, if I could, to make a creditable appearance.

Being now out of my time, I resolved to send down for my mother to come to me, believing it to be best for both, that no time might be lost. So I wrote the following letter to my parents:

———————————

Portsmouth, May 15, 1770.

"Hond. Father and Mother,

"I hope these few lines will find you both in perfect health, as I am at present, thanks be to God for it. I have the pleasure to let you

know I am out of my time, and live along with
Mrs. L___w, and shall be very glad if you will
come down and see me; which if you are in-
clined to do, pray write me word, and my an-
swer shall contain directions for the best road
you are to take. Pray give my kind love to
my brother and sister, and all friends that know
me. I conclude, with my prayers to God for
for you both,

    "your dutiful daughter,
    "MARY LACY.

    "P.S. DIRECT to me as follows:
"To William Chandler, at Mrs. Low's, in the
"Tree Rope-Walk, Portsmouth Common".

Next day as I lay in my bed, I heard the dock-bell ring, on
which I got up, and dressed myself as fast as I could, lest
I should be too late to the call. But notwithstanding the
haste I made, the bell still kept ringing, which raised my
wonder at the reason it rang so long. As soon as I came up
to the dock-wall I met a boatswain running with his coat
off, which made me conclude something very extraordi-

nary was the matter. When I came up to the dock gate, I found that all the yard was in a blaze, and the engines getting out; for the fire was so great and powerful that its heat almost resembled that of a furnacce: and I think I never in my life suffered so much for want of drink, as I did during the hurry and confusion it occasioned; the yard and taphouse being crowded with people, there was no getting any liquor.

While the fire was burning, a quarterman was dispatched to London with an account of it; and I was appointed to guard his house till he returned. After it was extinguished, we had orders to work a day and two tides; and were in a very great hurry at Portsmouth. The reason why I left Mrs. L___w was, because, after taking her for my friend, I at length discovered she had been all along the greatest enemy I ever had, having done many pitiful mean actions to me; but the betraying me exceeded all the rest, and was almost equal to the depriving me of life. It is most certain, she was an inveterate enemy to me, which she evidenced by endeavouring to do me all this disservice in her power, and that at a time when I was not possessed of a penny of money in the world, which I could call my own. However, all other injuries I should have regarded but little, if she had not discovered me to the men; for when

Mrs. F___s told me what I was, I fretted myself quite sick, and thought I should have broke my heart; but could not tell who she had told: and the apprehensions I felt from persons meddling with me, greatly affected me. So that by fretting and hard working, I was reduced very low, and thrown into a fit of illness; which those people who were ignorant of the real cause, construed to be love.

About this time an order came down for us to leave off working double tides, and only to work one day and two tides, which I was not sorry for; particularly on one account, as I was almost spent with working so close; for in a little time afterwards, I was seived with so bad a swelling in my thighs that I was not able to walk, and was unwilling the doctor should look at it, lest he should find me out: I therefore sent for the quarterman to answer for me that I was sick; which he accordingly did; and I continued a week before I was able to go into the yard again, and was then incapable of doing any work.

In a short time after I became better, and resumed my labour; after which we were ordered to go to Spithead to work, where we were in as bad a situation as before, having no other place to lie on but the softest plank we could find: so that such a wretched accommodation during that time made me catch cold again in my thighs, and occasioned my illness to return; however, I soon mended. But as the people were shifted about from one company to another, on the first of April I became very uneasy, less something disastrous should happen to me.

A short time after this, I was, on account of lameness, forced to go upon the doctor's list for a fortnight: but thank God I got the better of this, and went to work again, though continually apprehensive of being surprised unawares; for I did not know the particular persons my false friend had betrayed me to.

Soon afterwards our company was ordered to tear up an old forty gun ship, which was so very difficult to take to pieces that I strained my loins in an attempt; the effects of which I felt very sensibly at night when I went home, for I could hardly stand; and had no appetite to my victuals. But, notwithstanding my legs would scarce support me, I continued working till the ship was quite demolished, and then we were ordered on board the Sandwich, to bring on her waleing, which was very heavy. This increased my weakness to such a degree, that the going to work proved very irksome to me, insomuch that every body wondered what was the matter: however, I still continued my labour, till want of strength obliged me to quit it; and then I went to the doctor's shop, and told him I had strained my loins, which disabled me from working. Whereupon he gave me something which he thought would relieve me. I took it; but had it not been for the infinite mercy of God towards me, I should certainly have been killed by it, the medicine being altogether improper for my complaint; in consequence whereof, instead of growing better, I became every day worse than the former, which made me think I could not live long. However, in process of time my complaint abated, but not so as to enable me to work as I had done before, nor could I carry the same burdens as usual, which made me very uneasy.

While I continued in this weak condition, I imagined that if I could go down to Kent I might get a friend to help me out of the yard: but growing somewhat better, I went to work as well as I could. The loss of my father and mother like-wife greatly aggravated my concern; and I began to think of endeavouring to obtain liberty of the builder to go into Kent for a fortnight, which he readily granted. I went accordingly in one of the transports to Dover, from thence to Ash, and afterwards to the house of Mrs. Deverton, who was very much surprised at seeing me, and told me she had been up to London last week; and that her brother and sister at Kensington would be glad to see me.

On hearing this, I took my leave of Ash and set off for London; and when I came to Deptford, I met with William L___y, who was glad to see me. I told him I had got a letter for him from Betty S___e. I went home, and lay all night with him; for as I had done so before, I was not afraid of him. Having talked much to him about his girl, the next day he went with me to London; for I wanted to go to the Navy Office to get my liberty prolonged, where they told me I must come again some other day.

From the Navy Office my companion went with me to Kensington: but when I came there, I was apprehensive Mr. Richardson would betray me to the young man who did not know what I was: to prevent which, I immediately enquired for the gentleman's house; which being directed to, the people belonging to it informed me that he lived there; but I did not know any of them, as it was seventeen years since I had seen them before.

I told Mrs. Richardson that I had brought her a letter from Ash; and almost as soon as she had looked on it, she recollected who I was: but I desired her to be careful what she said before the young man, otherwise it would be the means of betraying me. She strictly complied with my request till he was gone. This was on Thursday; and I staid there until the Sunday night following, then set off; for I did not know that my liberty was renewed at the Navy Office. I got to Portsmouth on Monday; and I immediately informed the builder I was come back. Whereupon he told me that my liberty was renewed. However, I went to work; but was in a short time after taken as ill as ever.

As soon as I heard that Mrs. L___w had told everybody who I was, I was ready to break my heart; and immediately wrote to Mr. Richardson at Kensington, to desire him, if possible, to assist me. He sent me word he could not do any thing for me at that time, because all the gentlemen were out of town; but that in a month's time he would write, and let me know farther.

I endeavoured to keep up my spirits under these discouragements as well as I could; but still found the work proved harder and more fatiguing to me: Nor had I been from London a month before I was entered to the doctor's lift; for we had been putting the Sandwich in thorough repair, the working on which gave me such a pain in my side, that I was obliged to have a blister applied to it; and though the doctor's mate dressed it every day, he never discovered that I was a woman but often asked me why I did not marry.

In this condition I continued for some time; during which Mrs. L___w came from Woolwich. The very mention of this traitorous woman's name made me worse (for three or four days) than I was before. She had been but a short time in Portsmouth before Mr. Richardson sent for me to come up to Kensington; for as they new my father and mother, they were very much concerned about my welfare. This news in a few days gave a happy turn to my disorder, and almost restored me to health: so that I embraced the first opportunity of going over to Gosport, to take leave of them all; and went directly home to make myself ready to go with the coach.

My parting with the young women occasioned a scene of great perplexity and distress; and indeed one of them was ready to break her heart. This was poor Sarah, whose pitiable case affected me very much. However, I set off from Portsmouth the second day of December, 1771, and reached Kensington the next day; when Mr. Richardson advised me that the best step I could take was, to present a petition to the lords of the admiralty; which I accordingly did: and, their lordships, in consideration of my extraordinary sufferings and services, circumstanced as I was, have been so generous as to settle 20 *l.* a year upon me: for which, as in gratitude and duty bound, I shall pray for them as long as I live.

After the lords of the admiralty had granted my superannuated pension, I continued with the above mentioned Mr. Richardson as Kensington for about the space of ten months, during which time, on going to Deptford to receive my money, I was met by one Mr. Slade, who had removed thither from Portsmouth yard by order of the board. He has not seen me before in womens apparel; yet having heard of my metamorphosis, he enquired kindly after my health, and offered his service to conduct me back to Kensington.

On the road thither, he expressed a great affection for me; and at the same time requested me to give him my hand at the altar, allowing me a proper time to consider of his offer. Though I had repeatedly declared that I would remain single, yet afterwards having the utmost reason to believe that there subsisted a real and mutual affection betwixt us, and that the hand of Providence was engaged in bringing about our union, I at length gave my consent; in consequence of which, we were married, and now enjoy the utmost happiness the state affords; which I have the most sanguine hopes of a continuance of, since my husband is not only sober and industrious, but having been convinced, ever since the year 1762, of the important truths of Christianity, his conduct towards mankind in general, founded on a love of virtue, is upright and exemplary; at the same time that in his conjugal relation he behaves in the most endearing and indulgent manner. Thus united, I have, by the blessing of God, attained more than a bare chance for happiness in my present state, and have also the most solid grounds to look for the permanent enjoyment of it in future.